LINE
BY LINE
The Settle & Carlisle
25th Anniversary 1989 - 2014

Martin Buck   Foreword by Michael Portillo

FREIGHTMASTER

PUBLISHING

Contents

First published, April 2014:

Freightmaster Publishing
158 Overbrook
SWINDON
SN3 6AY

www.freightmasterpublishing.co.uk

ISBN : 978-0-9558275-8-7

Printed :

Stephens & George
Goat Mill Road
Dowlais
MERTHYR TYDFIL
CF48 3TD

www.stephensandgeorge.co.uk

Foreword

Over the last few years I have had many opportunities to admire the engineering achievements of the Victorian railway builders. Those who constructed the Settle to Carlisle line certainly deserve our praise. Indeed, many navvies were to lose their lives as a result of accidents, or because of the diseases that swept the workers' camps along the route. Rival railway companies had calculated that the London Midland would never be able to build a new route to Scotland between the east and west coast lines, given the challenging terrain and the hostile winter weather. They were wrong.

The line affords passengers sight of some of the most glorious scenery in England. But when you travel on the line, you are struck always by the large numbers of people standing close to the line to photograph the passing train, because they recognise that the railway enhances the natural beauty. Few can resist a sigh seeing a finely crafted image of a steam train crossing the Ribblehead viaduct. The valley would be magnificent without the railway surely. But the combination of nature and human artefact is breathtaking.

In the 1980s it seemed that the line might close. British Rail made an application to end services, and it fell to me as the minister of state for Transport to consider it. Our railways were losing money and the managers were under an obligation to find efficiencies. The numbers using the line had fallen sharply, and the Victorian viaducts were going to need large capital expenditure to keep them operational.

Fortunately, the case for closure was not an open and shut one. It emerged that the repairs could be done for a fraction of the original estimates. Also, with very few services per day, and few of the stations between Settle and Carlisle open, it was scarcely surprising that passenger numbers had fallen. What might the position be if all the stations were open (and well-tended) and if the frequency of trains increased? The Conservative government of which I was a member was concerned about pounds and pence; but it also had a respect for our national heritage. With imagination, the heritage could be protected, and the line radically improve its revenue.

The Friends of the Settle-Carlisle line assured me that they would mobilise the community and boost the passenger numbers if the line were spared. In the summer in which I had to decide, "suddenly" 350,000 people used the line, suggesting that the Friends' pledge was not mere bravado. It remains one of the happiest moments of my political career when I wrote to the organisation announcing my decision to reject British Rail's application for closure.

What has happened since has given me great joy. The stations along the line are enchanting, and they have opened up the hinterland to tourists and hikers, as well as improving hugely access to and from the villages. The numbers of passengers now travelling on the line has dwarfed those of twenty years ago.

One result of keeping the line open has been the increase in freight traffic, as heavily laden trains use the route in preference to the congested mainlines to east and west. So the line has a strategic importance, quite apart from its role in supporting local communities and tourism.

If I have a remaining hope it is that on the regular diesel services the operator might one day introduce rolling stock with a glass roof. It is such a pleasure on mountainous tracks on the continent to be in a properly-designed observation car, and the unusual rolling stock provides a powerful advertisement to potential passengers that a very special train journey is on offer. The managers of the regular train services today perhaps need to show some of the imagination that enabled the line to be saved twenty years ago.

Michael Portillo

Introduction

Welcome to this special edition of *"Line By Line"*, celebrating the 25th Anniversary of that momentous day in May 1989 when the historic Settle & Carlisle railway route ('S & C') was saved from closure. To mark the occasion, I have assembled a selection of superb images to illustrate the line in all its glory, by way of the locos, rolling stock and services associated with it. There's also a small selection of my own photographs (pre-1989) to provide a contrast.

Our journey to Carlisle does not actually start at Settle Junction, but just over three miles away at Hellifield, a station renowned for its superb Midland Railway architecture, an operational base for steam hauled charters and from where many travellers set out on their own journey.

The 'S & C' has become a very important railway route; a major freight artery (especially for Anglo-Scottish coal trains), diversionary route when the West Coast Main Line is blocked and a renowned 'heritage' railway, bringing rail enthusiasts and travellers from all over the world to sample its magic.

All this would not have been possible without the foresight and determination shown by the Government of the day and, in particular, the Right Honourable Michael Portillo, who saw the benefits of saving the line for the nation. The rest, as they say, is history!

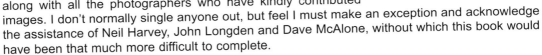

Michael Portillo *(right)* is now a familiar sight on British television, taking to the tracks with a copy of George Bradshaw's Victorian Railway Guidebook, travelling the length and breadth of the country to see how the railways changed Britain.

"Great British Railway Journeys" was first broadcast on BBC 2 in 2010, followed by further series, including travelling on the great train routes of Europe, retracing journeys featured in George Bradshaw's 1913 Continental Railway Guide.

I would like to thank Michael for writing the foreword for this title along with all the photographers who have kindly contributed images. I don't normally single anyone out, but feel I must make an exception and acknowledge the assistance of Neil Harvey, John Longden and Dave McAlone, without which this book would have been that much more difficult to complete.

There is also The Friends of the Settle - Carlisle Line (FOSCL) whose determination, inspiration and activities have helped promote the Settle & Carlisle for the benefit of us all. Formed way back in 1981 to campaign against the proposed closure of the line, since then they have acted as a user group to improve facilities and services for passengers.

This has resulted in many stations being reopened, more trains running, station buildings refurbished, platforms raised and Victorian style lamps installed. The disused signal boxes at Armathwaite and Settle have been restored and a 'Station Adoption Scheme' operates, whereby members tend the flower beds and look after the station's welfare.

The FOSCL, run by volunteers, produce and distribute promotional leaflets to boost passenger numbers, organise guided walks and work in partnership with other organisations on many projects.

This spirit sums up what the ' S & C' is all about and what it means to so many people.

Martin Buck

Swindon
April 2014

Legend

Schematic Diagrams

A profile of the route is given in 10-mile sections.

Gradient Profile

This is a 'cutaway' side-on-view, exaggerated sufficiently to show the changing gradients of the route. A vertical scale is shown in 200ft increments, rising to the summit of the line at Ais Gill, 1,169ft above sea level.

Track Plans

These are a 'birds eye' view of the route: running lines and junctions, stations, tunnels and viaducts clearly marked, although it should be noted that, while these plans are schematic and to scale, some features have been removed/enlarged to maintain clarity.

Key to Symbols

To make the diagrams easy to use, symbols and abbreviations have been kept to the absolute minimum. These are:

▬▬▬	station platform (in use)	**U.G.L.**	Up Goods loop
▭	station platform (disused)	**D.G.L.**	Down Goods Loop
SB	signal box	**U.P.L.**	Up Passenger Loop
PSB	power signal box	**D.P.L.**	Down Passenger Loop
....	trackbed	⋮	Boundary between signal box areas

All schematic diagrams originally created by **Mark Rawlinson**.

Signalling Notes

a) Signal boxes:

Settle signal box is still in situ, preserved, but no longer operational.

Armathwaite signal box is still in situ, preserved, no longer operational.

b) The 'Up' and 'Down' running lines between signal boxes were controlled by 'Absolute Block Section' signalling, resulting in some long sections of the route (for example, 10 miles between Garsdale and Kirkby Stephen) where only one train at a time could be in a section. This caused major pathing problems as the line became busier.

However, since 1989, colour light signals have been installed in some sections to become 'Intermediate Block Sections' (IBS), thus allowing more than one train occupation between signal boxes, notably:

- 'Up' and 'Down' IBS between Settle Junction and Blea Moor.
- 'Up' IBS between Garsdale and Kirkby Stephen.
- 'Up' IBS between Kirkby Stephen and Appleby.
- 'Up' and 'Down' IBS between Culgaith and Low House Crossing.

Setting the Scene

Background History

The Midland Railway always wanted to provide a through route to Scotland for its passengers. This came to fruition when the Settle & Carlisle opened for business in 1875 for freight traffic, followed by the first Midland passenger trains to run over their own metals on 1st May 1876.

Beforehand, after Skipton, the Midland Railway worked an independent line (nicknamed the Little North Western) to Carnforth and from Clapham Junction, the line branched off to Ingleton, where it made an end-on junction with a branch of the LNWR coming south from Low Gill on the WCML. This route proved unsatisfactory and the Company set out to have its own line from Settle Junction to Carlisle; work on this line started in 1869.

Construction

The line was built at very high cost and with great difficulty due to the terrain, involving heavy tunneling and bridgework. However, the Midland was undeterred and accorded the project the utmost priority in its attempt to forge its own slice of the Anglo-Scottish Market.

Construction took 6 years to complete, involving 6,000 workmen, and cost nearly £3.5 million. Its legacy is a remarkable feat of engineering, borne out by a few staggering facts:

- *Ais Gill* : summit of the line at 1,167ft and 250ft higher than Shap Summit on the WCML.
- *Ribblehead viaduct* : 24 arches, 440 yards long and 100ft high.
- *Dent station* : the highest main line station in England at 1,100 ft above sea level.
- *Garsdale* : the site of the highest water troughs in the world.

Passenger Operations

When the Midland Railway merged with the LNWR in 1923 to form the London Midland & Scottish Railway (LMS), it became apparent that the Midland route could not compete with the West Coast route in terms of speed, steeper gradients and greater length of journey. For example, in the early 1960s, the famous 'Thames Clyde Express' needed almost nine hours to complete the journey from London to Glasgow, compared with a faster time of just over seven hours from London Euston to Glasgow over the WCML.

The LMS, therefore, decided to concentrate on the WCML at the expense of the 'S & C'.

In its heyday, the important trains were the Anglo-Scottish expresses from London St. Pancras to Glasgow and Edinburgh; the *'Thames Clyde Express'* and the *'Waverley'*, respectively, providing a through service to Scotland for passengers in the East Midlands and Yorkshire.

The 'Midland Route' from London St Pancras to Glasgow was always problematical, expresses having to run through three regions (Midland, Eastern and Scottish) with loco changes en route at stations, such as Nottingham, Leeds and Carlisle; some regions were even reluctant to provide a new loco for a train originating in another region!

Decline

While the Settle & Carlisle did survive Dr Beeching, all stations except Settle and Appleby were closed from May 1970 and its passenger service cut to two trains a day in each direction, leaving mostly freight. The writing was well and truly on the wall ....

Few express passenger services continued to operate. The 'Waverley' from London St Pancras to Edinburgh ended in 1968, while the 'Thames-Clyde Express' from London to Glasgow Central lasted until 1975. Overnight sleepers from London to Glasgow continued until 1976, after that was a residual, daytime service from Glasgow, albeit cut back to Nottingham with three trains each way. These survived until 1982, when they were taken off the 'S & C' to run via Manchester and the WCML.

As for freight traffic, this ceased running over the 'S & C' in 1983.

In 1984, the Government and British Rail gave formal notice of its intention to close the 'S & C'. There was outrage; local authorities and rail enthusiasts joined forces to save the line, pointing out British Rail was ignoring the line's tourism potential, the need of a diversionary route for the West Coast Main Line, and failing to promote through traffic from the Midlands and Yorkshire to Scotland.

The campaign uncovered evidence that British Rail had mounted a 'dirty tricks' campaign, by exaggerating the cost of repairs (£6 million for Ribblehead Viaduct alone) and diverting traffic away from the line to justify its closure plans, a process referred to as **"closure by stealth"**.

However, when closure notices were posted on the remaining stations, the reverse effect was actually achieved with increased passenger numbers - rising from 93,000 in 1983 to 450,000 by 1989. In conjunction with local authorities, eight of the closed stations were reopened. Ironically, as BR did not wish to invest in new trains for the line, a combination of first-generation DMUs (used on local stopping trains) and Class 31s / Class 47s (hauling the 'faster' expresses), generated added interest and revenue, especially amongst rail enthusiasts.

Saviour

In 1989, however, the Right Honourable Michael Portillo, Minister of Transport, announced that closure was being declined as a result of the great public interest shown in the line and that the actual cost of repairing Ribblehead viaduct would be considerably less than originally anticipated. It was also hoped the great public interest displayed in saving the line could be turned into a means of creating greater posterity for the Settle & Carlisle.

Since then, the 'S & C' has gone from strength to strength and now all that remains, is to invite you to turn the page and enjoy one of the great railway journeys in the world.

Class 60 No.60074 'Teenage Spirit' (above), in blue livery promoting the Teenage Cancer Charity, passes Smardale on 19th March 2008 with 6E13, the 12:40 Newbiggin - Milford Sidings empty gypsum. **John Longden**

FREIGHT FLOWS

TIMELINE (1989 onwards - a potted history)

1994 - Gypsum

This was the flow that started a renaissance in freight traffic over the 'S & C'.

Desulphogypsum is produced by a new flue gas desulphurisation plant at Drax power station, which can be used to manufacture plasterboard. This also proved very cost efficient as desulphogypsum is a waste by-product and can be used instead of mined gypsum.

Trainloads of gypsum would be moved from Drax to the British Gypsum plant at Newbiggin, Kirkby Thore, conveyed in 20ft containers housed on a variety of wagons. These wagons include 'KFAs' built by Rautaruukki (Finland) in 1994, former Cawoods 2-axle 'PFAs', plus some EWS 'FBA' and 'FCA' wagons. Gypsum flows continue to this day.

The new train service was 'booked' for Immingham-based Class 60 traction (FDAI Pool).

6D89, 05:11 Drax ps - Newbiggin

1995 - Coal

In August 1995, freight operator 'Transrail' secured a contract with British Fuels to carry containerised coal from Gascoigne Wood to Inverness, hauled by a Class 37 / 56 loco, made up of British Fuel's own distinctive re-liveried containers. This working set out during daylight hours and provided a welcome source of new traffic over the 'S & C', albeit running only once a week. Unfortunately, this flow ceased running in 2000.

6M90, 16:48 (SO) Gascoigne Wood - Mossend

1997 - Coal

This was an important year for the Settle & Carlisle. It marked the start of regular Anglo-Scottish MGR (Merry Go Round) coal trains over the line to English power stations. The former British Steel import terminal at Hunterston on the Ayrshire coast, having been dormant since 1993 following the demise of iron ore traffic to Ravenscraig, re-opens.

Under Clydeport management, imported coal goes via the ex- Glasgow & South Western route to Carlisle and then over the 'S & C'. The first flow is:

6Z30, 11:55 Hunterston - Drakelow ps

This service was worked by a Toton-based Class 60 loco and, from this humble beginning, the number of MGR coal flows gradually increased to become the major commodity carried by the line.

English, Scottish & Welsh Railways (EWS) would ultimately enjoy a monopoly of coal services until Freightliner Heavy Haul enter the market in 2002. EWS used the iconic 2-axle ('HAA') 'Merry-go-Round' coal hoppers to transport the coal, replaced from 2000 onwards by new 'HTA' Bogie Coal Hoppers.

A sample timetable is reproduced on Page 11, showing passing freight recorded at Blea Moor on Friday, 8th March 2013, which clearly shows the amount of coal traffic running over the 'S & C'.

2002 - Coal

From March, Freightliner Heavy Haul (FHH) commence running coal trains over the Settle & Carlisle using their own Polish-built 'HHA' bogie hoppers, which were already being used on internal coal flows in England.

FHH would go on to increase their market share of the Anglo-Scottish coal market, running as many coal trains over the 'S & C' as their main competitor, EWS.

The initial loaded services were:

6Z39, 21:48 New Cumnock - Drax ps
6Z41, 21:40 Hunterston - Rugeley ps

2002 - Departmental

In July, the daily engineer's (departmental) service from Crewe to Carlisle, diagrammed for a Class 56 loco, starts running over the 'S & C' instead of the West Coast Main Line, even though the return working (6K05) to Crewe still runs via the WCML. This service transfers wagons, equipment and materials required for infrastructure work on the rail network. The service is:

6C02, 04:23 Crewe Basford Hall - Carlisle Yard

This service ultimately reverts back to WCML running in March 2005, which is still the case today. Interestingly, the return service (6K05) goes over to the 'S & C' in March 2009!

2004 - Cement

The Lafarge cement terminal at Brunthill (Carlisle) starts to receive cement in bagged form, transported in Cargowaggons, from Earles Sidings via the 'S & C' in the Hope Valley and from Oxwellmains in Scotland, transported from there in 2-axle 'PCA' cement tanks. The terminal can also receive the cement from Earles in 'PCAs'.

The new service commences in February and runs on a weekly basis, on either a Tuesday or Thursday. The train is hauled by a FHH Class 66/5 loco and the reporting details are:

6M38, 04:30 Earles Sidings - Carlisle Brunthill (loaded)

This service ran until February 2006.

2007 - Plasterboard

Perhaps not quite as headline-grabbing as the launch of the DRS operated 'Tesco Express' but, nevertheless, a new and innovative service. This service starts in July 2007 conveying plasterboard from the British Gypsum works at Kirkby Thore (Newbiggin) to Elderslie, near Paisley, in Scotland. The service ran as:

4S39, 00:34 Newbiggin - Elderslie

This train was formed of 'Megafret' flat wagons, carrying canvas 'Curtainsiders', sporting the British Gypsum logo and corporate colours. Unfortunately, this flow was short-lived!

2008 - Cement

Cement from Clitheroe to Scotland (Gunnie) ceased running in December 1992, when the train was worked by 2 x Class 37 locos, albeit via the West Coast Main Line (WCML).

A new thrice-weekly service begins, which sees an EWS Class 66/0 loco running from the Castle Cement works at Horrocksford (Clitheroe) to Scotland, using purpose built 'JPA' bogie cement wagons. The new service runs as:

6S00, 17:11 (WFO) Clitheroe - Mossend

2008 - Sand

In July, EWS operate a trial trainload of sand from Carlisle to Leeds using ex-National Power 'JMA' and 'JHA' hoppers. The sand originates from Tarmac Northern's Cardewmires Quarry, near Dalston, and loaded onto rail at Carlisle London Road. The reporting details for this short-lived service are.

6Z71, 09:56 Carlisle London Road - Leeds Hunslet

Short Term (STP) stone flows from both Ribblehead and Shap Quarry still run to Leeds Hunslet today, albeit very infrequently.

2009 - Departmental

The daily (return) departmental service from Carlisle Yard to Crewe switches to running over the 'S & C' in March, hauled by one of the ubiquitous EWS Class 66/0 locos. It is one of the more 'reliable' train services, as it runs nearly every day and is a good time-keeper.

6K05, 12:26 Carlisle Yard - Crewe Basford Hall

Although this service can occasionally run as a light engine (0K05), when there is no payload with which to go south, it can be a very interesting service in terms of wagons and locos ....

The train can include a variety of 2-axle and bogie open box, hopper and flat wagons, which carry:

- track hardware (crossovers, rails, sleepers, etc)
- plant machinery (cranes, diggers, tractors, etc)
- materials (ballast, spoil, stone, etc)

Furthermore, this service can also be seen with more than one loco at the head of the train, as 6K05 is used as a means of re-positioning locos between Carlisle and Crewe. This is a practical solution to eliminate costly light engine moves (see image on Page 29).

From August 2013, responsibility for providing motive power for this particular service (and outward 6C02) switches from DBS (DB Schenker) to DRS (Direct Rail Services).

2010 - Timber

The introduction of this new service would probably win the award for the most colourful and exciting of all the new flows to grace the 'S & C' in recent times, both in terms of consist and motive power.

Timber from the forests in Northern England and Scotland has been moved by rail to the Kronospan MDF manufacturing factory in Chirk for many years. However, from January 2010, a new freight operator moves into the market - *Colas Rail* - who operate a dedicated timber flow (taking over from Amec Spie Rail) using converted 'KFA' Cargowaggons. Traction would be in the shape of a Colas Class 66/8 loco. This service can also run via the West Coast main Line.

6J37, 12:29 Carlisle Yard - Chirk

From August, Colas secure another contract from Kronospan, this time moving timber from a loading point alongside Ribblehead station to Chirk; the empty timber carriers moving to the site via Carlisle Upperby, the 'S & C' or WCML and a reversal at Hellifield.

6Z41, 19:05 (FO) Ribblehead - Chirk

The new service was initially allocated a Colas Class 47 loco and, once the timber carriers arrived at Ribblehead, the loco would run light engine (0Z41) to Crewe, returning when the timber had been loaded. This traffic runs as required.

2010 - Coal

In July, railfreight operator GBRf started moving imported coal from the bulk import terminal at Hunterston to Drax power station, using their own 'HYA' bogie coal hoppers. What was interesting about this flow is that whilst the loaded train was routed from Carlisle via the Tyne Valley and ECML, the returning empties were routed via the 'S & C'.

4S51, 07:45 Drax ps - Hunterston

At present, any GBRf Anglo-Scottish coal services are no longer routed this way, loaded or empty, and run via the East Coast Main Line and / or the Tyne Valley instead.

(Opposite) : Coal is the principal commodity carried over the Settle & Carlisle, originating from opencast mines in Ayrshire and the Hunterston Bulk Import Terminal. A combination of 'S & C' elements; fells, cloud and dramatic lighting greet DBS Class 66/0 No.66118, as an incredibly lucky window of sunlight pierces the gloom to highlight the bright red loco. No.66118 works south through Shaw Paddock with 6E77, Hunterston - West Burton coal.   John Longden

Freight Traffic Survey

Blea Moor

Friday, 8th March 2013

From a humbling beginning of a solitary gypsum service in 1994, the volume of freight traffic has increased significantly and will, hopefully, continue to do so. To compensate for a dwindling number of paths on the busy West Coast Main Line, freight operators have been turning to the 'S & C' for additional paths to run their trains.

Anglo-Scottish MGR coal traffic to English power stations has grown to become the staple diet of freight on the Settle & Carlisle, as can be seen from the following observations of passing freight trains at Blea Moor on Friday, 8th March 2013:

Time	Direction	Code	Origin	Destination	Commodity
01:30	(South)	6E72	New Cumnock	Ferrybridge	coal
01:55	(South)	6E74	New Cumnock	Drax	coal
03:15	(South)	6M14	New Cumnock	Ratcliffe	coal
05:15	(North)	4S34	Leeds Hunslet	Hunterston	coal empties
06:00	(North)	4S66	Milford	Greenburn	coal empties
06:35	(North)	4S84	Milford	New Cumnock	coal empties
08:15	(North)	4M20	West Burton	Newbiggin	gypsum
08:15	(South)	6E77	Hunterston	West Burton	coal
08:45	(South)	6E76	Hunterston	Cottam	coal
10:30	(North)	4S11	Drax	Killoch	coal empties
10:50	(South	4M00	Mossend	Clitheroe	cement empties
11:50	(South)	6E93	Hunterston	Ferrybridge	coal
12:20	(South)	6M11	Killoch	Fiddlers Ferry	coal
13:35	(South)	4B13	Newbiggin	West Burton	gypsum empties
14:25	(South)	6Z68	Killoch	Drax	coal
14:35	(South)	6K05	Carlisle Yard	Crewe B. H.	departmental
14:35	(North)	4S62	Milford	New Cumnock	coal empties
14:50	(South)	6J37	Carlisle Yard	Chirk	timber
17:00	(North)	4S93	Milford	New Cumnock	coal empties
18:35	(North)	6S00	Clitheroe	Mossend	cement
21:35	(South)	6Z71	Ravenstruther	Ratcliffe	coal
22:15	(South)	6E06	Hunterston	Cottam	coal

Via Blackburn (freight only and diverted WCML services) : On 25th March 2011, Colas Class 66/8 No.66843 (above) passes Hellifield Green with 6J37, the 12:29 Carlisle Yard - Chirk, loaded timber. The train is heading for Daisyfield Junction (Blackburn) on a line which sees less than a handful of scheduled freight services each way each day.

Routes to the 'Settle & Carlisle'

Before we can start our northbound journey from Hellifield, trains have to get there, which will either be from the WCML (via Blackburn) or through Airedale (via Skipton).

Via Skipton (freight and passenger) : Heading east and away from Hellifield, Riviera Trains Class 47/8 No.47847 (below) makes its way towards Skipton and Leeds with 6Z50, the 09:45 Carlisle Yard - Shirebrook on 2nd February 2007. The loco had been hired to take a rake of GE Rail Services 'KFA' bogie vans to W.H. Davis at Langwith Junction, Shirebrook, for conversion into timber carriers. **Neil Harvey (2)**

Keith McGovern

The Journey

Hellifield - Ais Gill - Carlisle

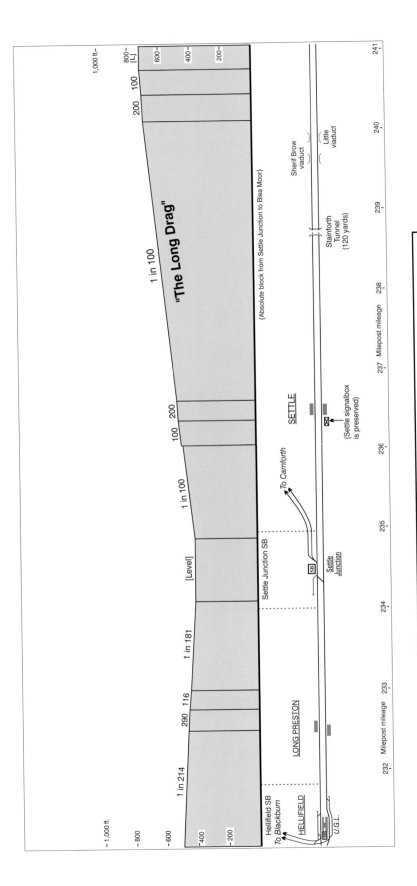

Hellifield - Horton in Ribblesdale

HELLIFIELD : FHH Class 66/5 No.6657 (above) passes Hellifield on 23rd March 2003 with 4Z42, the 14:00 (Sun) York Holgate – Ravenstruther empty 'HHA' coal hoppers. Coal trains running over the Settle & Carlisle on a Sunday were, and still are, a rare event. **Martin Buck**

HELLIFIELD

The original station was opened by the 'Little' North Western Railway in 1849, which was followed by a larger replacement (the current station) built by the Midland Railway, opening on 1 June 1880. It is situated immediately to the north of the junction of the line from Leeds and the newly completed Lancashire & Yorkshire Railway route from Blackburn via Clitheroe.

By the late 1980s, the main buildings and canopies were in very poor condition and under threat of demolition but, following a £500,000 cash injection between British Rail, English Heritage and the Railway Heritage Trust, they were refurbished. The ornate canopies are original Midland Railway design.

The last remaining signal box is at Hellifield South Junction, a Midland Railway Type 4c design, opening on 11th June 1911 and fitted with a Midland Railway Tappet lever frame. This replaced an 1880s-built signal box and now controls the signals in the station area along with the station approaches from the direction of Settle Junction, Clitheroe and Leeds.

The signal box became just 'Hellifield' in March 1966 after concentration of the signalling to this one location, allowing Hellifield North Junction signal box to close.

Operations : The line from Blackburn lost its local passenger service in September 1962, but remained open for freight and West Coast Main Line diversions. Local trains to Carlisle ended in May 1970, although remaining to be served by expresses to & from Glasgow until 1975. It was then served only by stopping trains between Leeds and Morecambe.

Trains to and from Carlisle started calling again in May 1995 and Hellifield still remains a start & finish point for passengers using the 'S & C' and an operating base for steam charters.

(Top) : A couple of passengers head for the subway and the exit on 20th March 2009, after detraining at Hellifield from Class 158 No.158904 on the 14:49hrs Leeds - Carlisle.   **Dave McAlone**

(Above) : As the peg goes off for a westbound service, BR Large Logo Class 47/4 No.47443 'North Eastern' approaches Hellifield on 20th May 1989 with 1E28, the 12:37 Carlisle - Leeds.   **Neil Harvey**

Hellifield South Junction

A great shot showing both the signal box and 'diamond' crossing, which leads to the Blackburn line. On a dull and dreary 4th May 1996, Loadhaul, two-tone grey, Class 60 No.60064 'Back Tor' (above) takes the Leeds route with 6E13, the 13:25 Newbigginn - Drax containerised gypsum empties.   **Neil Harvey**

The signals mounted on the gantry in the foreground are the 'Up Home' semaphore (left) for the Leeds direction and the lower semaphore (right) for the 'branch', diverging to Clitheroe and Blackburn. Framed by this gantry, the 'Down Home' signal is 'off' for the passing of FHH Class 66/5 No.66565 (below) on 20th March 2009 with 4S68, the 15:05 Leeds - Killoch empty coal hoppers.   **Dave McAlone**

Long Preston

On a quiet Sunday afternoon in March 2003, Class 156s No.156488 + 156482 (above) enter Long Preston with 2H63, the 09:25 Carlisle - Leeds service. Note the low, staggered platforms of this LNWR station. The author's car (at the time), a Honda Prelude, looks decidedly small alongside the articulated trailer belonging to R.H.Newhouse of Settle parked in the station car park. **Martin Buck**

A quintessentially North Yorkshire landscape of drystone walled pastures. GBRf Class 66/7 No.66746 (below) approaches Back Lane, just west of Long Preston railway station, on 3rd May 2013 with 4B13, the 12:40 Newbiggin - West Burton. These containers are used to transport gypsum from English power stations to the British Gypsum plant at Newbiggin for use in the manufacture of plasterboard. **Neil Harvey**

SETTLE JUNCTION

This is where the LNWR line to Carnforth diverges and the start of the *'Long Drag';* 22 miles of almost continual climb to reach the summit at Ais Gill.

The first sod was cut near Settle Junction at Anley in November 1869, when it was not called Settle Junction and the line went straight on to Clapham. A station once stood at Settle Junction, opening in November 1876 and closing exactly one year later in November 1877.

On 1st May 1979, all 41 wagons of a St. Blazey - Carlisle Yard freight derailed at Settle Junction causing significant disruption to services using both the 'S & C' and LNWR line.

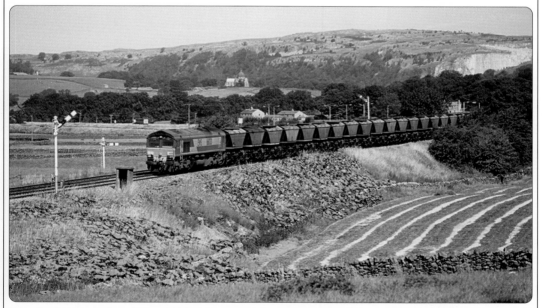

(Top) : Loadhaul Class 60 No.60007 passes Settle Junction on 2nd August 1996 with 6E13, the 13:25 Newbiggin - Milford gypsum empties; The mass of Pen-y-Ghent dominates the skyline.   **Neil Harvey**

(Above) : The grass in the pasture has been freshly cut as DBS Class 66/0 No.66020 picks up speed, having been given 'the road' with 6U51, the 06:20 Ayr Falkland Junction - Drax loaded coal. The train is formed of 'HAA'-style 2-axle hoppers fitted with a canopy.   **Martin Buck**

Storm clouds gather as Class 142 'Pacer' unit No.142095 (above) is about to join the main line off the 'Little North Western' line from Carnforth with the 12:58hrs Morecambe - Leeds. It's no exaggeration, but you can see how the 'S & C' begins to climb from this point onwards.   **Martin Buck**

Class 37/0 No.37116 'Sister Dora' (below) was a favourite with rail enthusiasts because of its non-standard blue 'Transrail' livery. Here it is working 6M90, the 16:48 (SO) Gascoigne Wood - Mossend containerised coal on 31st May 1997, just as a charter train passes in the opposite direction!   **Neil Harvey**

Meanwhile, on the penultimate Sunday of West Coast diversions in March 2003, Class 47/8 No.47854 (above) heads the first southbound service ; 1M64, 13:49 Carlisle - London Euston, and will shortly pass Settle Junction signal box situated on the 'Down' side of the line.　　　　　　**Martin Buck**

A few miles further north, just south of Settle, on 20th August 2012, Colas Rail Class 66/8s No.66848 and No.66849 'Wylam Dilly' (below) double head 6J37, the 12:44 Carlisle Yard - Chirk loaded timber, formed of 21 converted 'KFA' Cargowaggons. The sun just about stayed out long enough for the shot!　　　　**Neil Harvey**

SETTLE

Settle station was opened in 1876 and has one of the large Derby Gothic Style station buildings. All the stations on the Settle & Carlisle (except Culgaith) were designed by John Holloway Sanders and are of the style known as 'Derby Gothic'.

The Midland Railway Company required its buildings to be made of quality materials, local sandstone, Welsh slate, and massive oak roof trusses. There are three styles of building:

Type A : the largest - Appleby, Kirkby Stephen and Settle.

Type B : middle size - with wings either side of a single main building, eg. Langwathby.

Type C : smallest - have only a wing at one side. (eg. Ribblehead and Horton-in-Ribblesdale).

This is one of the three stations which originally served Settle, the other two were the original Settle (renamed Giggleswick in 1877) and Settle Junction, which closed in 1877. The station formed part of a larger complex including a goods shed, weigh office, sidings, cattle dock, signal box and water tank. Goods facilities were withdrawn in 1970.

Settle Station Signal Box opened on the 12th of April 1891, a standard timber-built 'Midland type 2a' design manufactured in kit form at the Midland Railway Company's signalling workshops in Derby. It closed for operational purposes in May 1984 and lay derelict for more than a decade. The signal box, owned by Network Rail, was given to the Friends of the Settle-Carlisle Line in June 1997, with the proviso it was re-sited and restored, which it was.

Settle station railwayana:

(Left) The old Midland Railway sign is now situated on the 'Up' platform, having previously been located in the middle of the 'twin arrows' featured below.

(Below) : The station has remained unchanged with flower beds and the famous 'twin arrow' sign. The original name boards have been replaced along with a new sign welcoming passengers to the Yorkshire Dales.   **Martin Buck (2)**

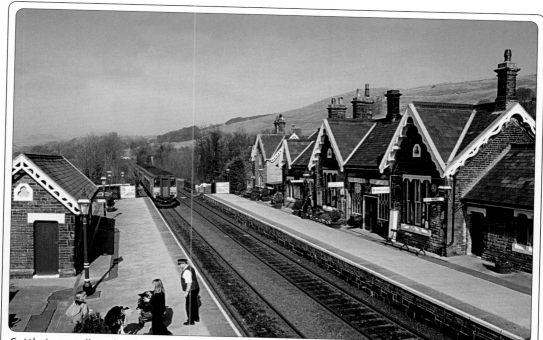

Settle is a small market town in North Yorkshire, historically in the West Riding of Yorkshire, believed to have 7th-century Anglian origins, its name being the Angle word for settlement.

Its beautifully maintained station building is here for all to see on a sunny Sunday, 23rd March 2003, as 2H64, the 13:01 Leeds - Carlisle service, formed of Nos.156488 + 156482 (above), heads away from the station after dropping off a couple of passengers; a friendly member of staff looks on in case his assistance is needed.

Martin Buck

Class 66/0 No.66111 (below) is a DBS 'shed' which has a Highland Stag logo on the body side. It is seen here passing under the station footbridge on 20th May 2010 with the southbound 4M00, 07:05 Mossend - Clitheroe 'Castle Cement' empties.

Neil Harvey

Langcliffe

After leaving Settle, the line climbs across Langcliffe embankment with Giggleswick Scar on the left and Langcliffe Scar on the right, before the line passes through a cutting to reach Stainforth.

On 28th April 2011, Class 66/0 No.66129 (above) climbs past Langcliffe with 6S00, the 17:05 Clitheroe - Mossend loaded cement, conveyed in VTG 'JPA' Bogie Cement Tank Wagons.

On the same day, but heading south, FHH Class 66/5 No.66555 (below) coasts downhill at Langcliffe with 6Z32, the 10:03 Killoch - Ratcliffe loaded coal.

Neil Harvey (2)

Sherif Brow

The railway courses the River Ribble to Ribblehead and across the river twice at Sherif Brow. The two viaducts are just 300 yards apart, the first one is (not surprisingly) called Sherif Brow Viaduct followed by Little Viaduct. On 5th May 2007, Virgin 'Thunderbird' Class 57/3 No.57316 'Fab 1' (above) is seen at Sherif Brow with 1S63, the diverted 13:00 London Euston - Glasgow Central.   **Neil Harvey**

Helwith Bridge

Taken from a lower angle to get more of the blue sky in above the loco, DRS Class 66/4 No.66421 (below) rattles downgrade towards Helwith Bridge on 19th May 2011 with 6J37, the 12:18 Carlisle Yard - Chirk 'logs', and yet another loco / livery type for this working! Until 1969, granite was quarried here by the Helwith Bridge Granite Co., which had sidings on the 'down' side of the line.   **John Longden**

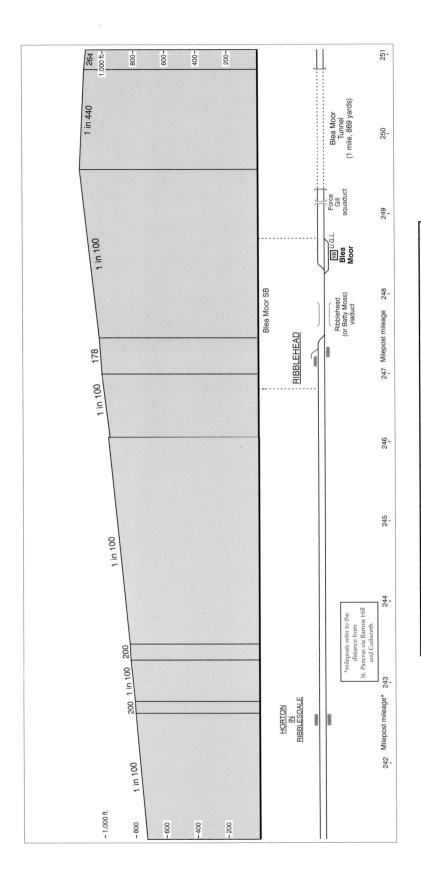

Horton in Ribblesdale - Dent Head

Selside : A super broadside view is captured of two-tone grey Class 60 No.60013 'Robert Boyle', (above) as it passes Selside on 14th April 2007 with an early-running 6E16, 17:34 Newbiggin – Milford Sidings gypsum empties.　**Neil Harvey**

Horton-in-Ribblesdale

Class 47/4 No.47455 (above) heads south through Horton-in-Ribblesdale on 25th April 1987, two years before the decision is made to save the line from closure, with 1E33, the 16:15 Carlisle - Leeds. Horton station closed on 4th May 1970, but the station building on the 'up' platform is still visible, as is the redundant signal box; the top of which can just be made out above the fifth coach.

Selside

The railway passes Selside on an embankment leading up to Ribblehead, in an area notable for limestone pavements and caves, the most famous being Alum Pot. Having waited patiently for some sun (to no avail!), a shot is gained of two Class 37s No.37108 + 37509 (below) on 6M90, the 16:48 Milford - Mossend containerised coal at 8pm on 29th June 1996 - with a train that only runs once a week, it's pot luck if you obtain a favourable result. There used to be a signal box at Selside, which closed in 1975. **Neil Harvey (2)**

Salt Lake Cottages

Having reached 1,000 feet, the line passes the cottages at Salt Lake, so named after the shanty town that once stood here during construction of the Settle & Carlisle. Whilst this has long gone, Midland cottages, like others found beside the line, still remain. On 20th May 2010, GBRf Class 66/7 No.66706 ' Nene Valley' (above) passes Salt Lake with 4S21, the 07:20 Drax - New Cumnock coal empties - pity the loaded train was not routed this way too.

Neil Harvey

Could this picture set a record for the most locos captured moving on the 'S & C' at one time? Five locos in one shot! Either way, it makes for very interesting viewing as Class 66/0 No.66016 (below), with Nos. 66182, 66201 and 66147 all DIT ('Dead In Tow'), leads a lengthy 6K05, 12:18 Carlisle Yard - Crewe Basford Hall on 11th October 2010 past Salt Lake Cottages. In the other direction, Colas Rail Class 47/7 No.47739 'Robin of Templecombe' works light engine to Ribblehead to collect loaded timber wagons.

John Longden

Ribblehead Timber

Timber Traffic : August 2010 sees the start of timber being moved by rail from Ribblehead to the Kronospan factory at Chirk. The timber is felled in the nearby Langstrothdale area around Greenfield. On a very wet 7th September 2012, Colas Class 66/8 No.66849 (above) sits at Ribblehead while its train is loaded with logs to form 6Z70, the 14:14 (FO) Ribblehead - Chirk.
Keith McGovern

Colas Rail Class 47/7 No.47739 'Robin of Templecombe' works the first trainload of timber from Ribblehead in August 2010. Two months later, 27th October 2010, No.47739 (below) heads towards Blea Moor to run round, so it can then proceed south with 4Z41, the 19:05 (FO) Ribblehead - Chirk.
Ross Byers

56302

Class 66/0 No.66006 accelerates north through Ribblehead station on 31st May 2013 with 4S62, the 11:27 ...lford - New Cumnock empty coal hoppers. Colas Class 56 No.56302 (above), meanwhile, shunts in the ...dings at Ribblehead prior to departing with that afternoon's timber train to Chirk.

...ving now run round its train at Blea Moor, No.56302 (below) starts off and retraces its steps to pass ...bblehead station again, about 40 minutes early, with 6Z70, Ribblehead - Chirk loaded timber wagons. ...is was the first time a Class 56 had worked this particular diagram. **Steven Brykajlo (2)**

Ribblehead

Ribblehead station originally closed in May 1970 but reopened in 1986. It now has staggered platforms, which was not always the case. The 'down' platform was reinstated in 1993 after it was removed to make way for a new siding so, in the early 1980s, trains could only call in the southbound direction!

In previous years, Ribblehead served as a meteorological station, with the stationmaster transmitting coded reports to the Air Ministry. Beforehand, in the 1870s, monthly services were held in the station's waiting room by the Vicar of Ingleton, accompanied by a harmonium concealed behind a billboard in the waiting room. This musical instrument had been brought to the station by a missionary who came as a minister to the construction gangs when the railway was being constructed.

The former signal box closed in 1969, located on the down side of the line, and the adjacent siding once served Ribblehead Quarry, now a nature reserve.

After the station, the line reaches the most famous location on the Settle & Carlisle - Ribblehead (or Batty Moss) Viaduct - the main focus of attention and one of the main reasons cited in favour of closure of the entire route; namely, costly repairs to the structure, which we all now know was somewhat spurious! Fortunately, common sense prevailed.

The viaduct may be the most written about or photographed structure on the Settle & Carlisle, and why not, as one cannot but be amazed at its majesty. What can one say, but repeat a few well known statistics to illustrate its magnificence:

- the viaduct has 24 arches
- is 106 feet high
- is 440 yards in length
- took 5 years to build between 1870 and 1875.
- built from local limestone
- the spoil from Blea Moor Tunnel was used to form the northern embankment.

From the viaduct, there are splendid views of the Yorkshire Three Peaks: Pen-y-ghent (2,277ft), Ingleborough (2,373ft) and the highest of the three, Whernside (2,419ft), which dominates high above desolate Blea Moor.

The entrance to the siding can be seen alongside the running lines at Ribblehead station, where DBS Class 66/0 No.66138 (above) heads along the 'Up 'platform line on 2nd June 2007 with 6E85, the 05:00 Hunterston - Drax coal, loaded in 'HTAs'. **Neil Harvey**

(Opposite) : The snow lies crisp and even at Ribblehead station and, unsurprisingly, there are no passengers waiting for the 13:20hrs train service to Leeds on 16th January 2013. **Ross Byers**

Meanwhile, having crossed the viaduct on 23rd August 2008, No.66034 (below) approaches Ribblehead station with 6Z71, the 10:27 Carlisle Yard - Leeds Hunslet sand train, which only ran three times. Fortunately, a shot was obtained, as the smart looking 'JMA' Bogie Coal hoppers are a rare sight on the Settle & Carlisle. The bogie hoppers were ordered initially by National Power - hence the blue livery - for use on MGR coal trains from Gascoigne Wood to Drax and limestone from Tunstead. **Neil Harvey**

Batty Moss - *"Take 4"*

Worth the climb? This super shot provides an unusual, bird's eye view of the viaduct along with Ribblehead quarry in the background, as seen from the top of Whernside on 9th September 1997. An unidentified Class 60 (above) heads north across the viaduct with 6G82, the 10:40 Drax - Newbiggin loaded gypsum.

A colourful Class 47/4 No.47595 'Confederation of British Industry' (below) and its rake of coaches looks impressive as it crosses Ribblehead Viaduct with 1E01, the 06:30 Carlisle - Leeds on 25th June 1988.

Although both traction and rolling stock have changed over the years, fortunately, little else has; the viaduct is still standing and the dry-stone walls are still a dominant feature in the fields in this part of the world. On 18th June 2012, Class 66/0 No.66016 (above) crosses Batty Moss viaduct at 18:19hrs with the northbound loaded cement - 6S00, 17:05 Clitheroe - Mossend.   **Keith McGovern**

In dramatic early morning light, giving strong earth tones, EWS Class 66/0 No.66130 (below) and 21-loaded 'HTAs' cross the viaduct on 10th December 2008 with 6E77, the 01:00 Hunterston - Drax. Snow-capped Whernside is prominent in the background.   **Neil Harvey (3)**

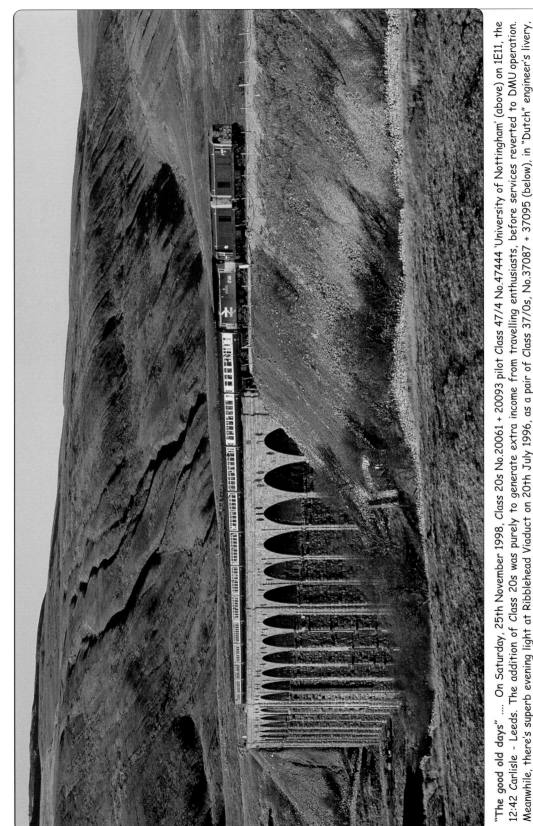

"The good old days" .... On Saturday, 25th November 1998, Class 20s No.20061 + 20093 pilot Class 47/4 No.47444 'University of Nottingham' (above) on 1E11, the 12:42 Carlisle - Leeds. The addition of Class 20s was purely to generate extra income from travelling enthusiasts, before services reverted to DMU operation. Meanwhile, there's superb evening light at Ribblehead Viaduct on 20th July 1996, as a pair of Class 37/0s, No.37087 + 37095 (below), in "Dutch" engineer's livery, head north with 6M90, the 16:48 Gascoigne Wood - Carlisle Yard coal, conveyed in British Fuels containers. For a time in the late 1990s, this was the 'top' freight

BLEA MOOR

(Above) : Loadhaul Class 60 No.60007 passes Blea Moor on 16th August 1996 with loaded 2-axle 'HAA' MGR coal hoppers running from Carlisle Yard to Eggborough power station.   **Neil Harvey**

(Below) : Zooming in, the track layout at Blea Moor is clearly discernible as 'shed' No.66100 passes Blea Moor signal box with 6K05, the 12:18 Carlisle Yard - Crewe Basford Hall departmental on 18th June 2012, proceeding cautiously along the 'Up Main' for the run across Ribblehead Viaduct.   **Keith McGovern**

(Above) : On 29th May 2009, Class 66/0 No.66091 passes Blea Moor with 6M00, the 07:03 Mossend - Clitheroe cement empties formed of 13 'Castle Cement' 100 Tonne 'JPA' wagons, some of which are still in grey livery and yet to be branded 'Castle Cement'. **Neil Harvey**

(Below) : After arriving at Ribblehead at 06:05hrs and walking up to Blea Moor, this was the first freight to be seen on the day. On a glorious 18th June 2012, GBRf's recently acquired FHH Class 66/5 loco, now numbered No.66740 but still in green, heads for Blea Moor tunnel with 4M20, the 02:51 West Burton - Newbiggin loaded gypsum. The 2,373ft mass of Ingleborough looms in the background. **Keith McGovern**

BLEA MOOR

Blea Moor signal box is one of the most remote and lonely signal boxes in Great Britain, just under a mile from the nearest road and lying in the shadow of Whernside, 2,419ft high. It is so remote that, by way of example, in the late 1970s and early 1980s, two daily freight services running between Carlisle and Tinsley (7E84 / 8M18) stopped at the signal box to set down water cans for the signalman and to pick up the empties!

The signal box is a London, Midland and Scottish Railway (LMS) type 11c, fitted with a 30 lever Railway Executive Committee frame. It opened on 16th December 1941, replacing a 1914-built signal box located on the down side of the line 70 yards to the north. This took place when the 'Down lie-by' siding and the 'No1 Up lie-by' siding were converted into 'Down' and 'Up' goods loops, respectively. The 'Down' loop is now out of use.

The original LMS post-1935 design nameboard was replaced by a locally made nameboard in the mid 1980s and the signal box was fitted with uPVC windows in the early 2000s.

After passing the signal box, the line enters a cutting, crossing Force Gill before Force Gill crosses over the line itself on a purpose-built aqueduct, before plunging into the depths of Blea Moor Tunnel.

Blea Moor Tunnel took five years to build between 1870 - 1875 and is 2,629 yards in length; twice as long as the second longest tunnel on the route at Rise Hill. It passes some 500 feet below Blea Moor and was built with the aid of seven ventilation shafts from the moor above, of which only three are still in use today. About mid-way in the tunnel, the line crosses the county boundary between North Yorkshire and Cumbria.

Blea Moor Signal Box : Front-on view (above) taken on 19th June 2012.   **Keith McGovern**

Blea Moor Tunnel (South Portal) is not such a popular choice among photographers compared to the northern exit of the tunnel; perhaps due to the south portal being quite a trek after leaving your car below the arches of Ribblehead Viaduct or in the car park of the 'Station Inn' hostelry.

Nevertheless, the south portal does make an interesting compositon, especially as spoil from the tunnel's construction is still visible in places on the hillside above. On 19th June 2013, FHH Class 66/6 No.66604 (opposite) emerges from the south portal with 6E73, the 04:45 Hunterston - Cottam loaded coal. Note the date of opening '1874' on the tunnel entrance.   **Neil Harvey**

Blea Moor Tunnel (North Portal)

Between October 2003 and September 2004, Arriva Trains Northern introduce a daily out & back loco-hauled diagram on the S & C, comprising a EWS Class 37/4 + 4 Arriva MkII vehicles + EWS Class 37/4. This proved to be a major attraction for both loco haulage enthusiasts and photographers alike, not to mention being a money-maker for Arriva too - pity it did not last! On 24th September 2004, No.37408 'Loch Rannoch' (above) leads 1M53, the 09:47 Leeds - Carlisle out of Blea Moor tunnel.   **Richard Armstrong**

This location is a popular choice among photographers and, perhaps, the best view is from a lower angle, as we see here. On 7th May 2008, Class 66/0 No.66156 (below) emerges from the north portal of the tunnel into a peaceful Dentdale with 6M20, the 04:30 Drax - Newbiggin loaded gypsum.   **John Longden**

Dent Head

This view at Dent Head has a nice seasonal feel to it as more and more cloud cover arrives in Dentdale from the west. A grimy DRS Class 66/4 No.66430 (above) brings up the rear of an equally grimy train set with No.66424 leading 3J11, the Carlisle Kingmoor Railhead Treatment Train (RHTT) on 24th October 2013. The train is crossing 'Dales Way', which links Dent with the main Ingleton - Hawes (B6255) road.   **John Longden**

From a more elevated vantage point, DBS Class 66/0 No.66079 'Benjamin Gimbert GC' (below) is seen on the approach to the tunnel on 28th July 2012 with 6L41, Carlisle Yard- Gisburn engineer's train. The consist includes 'YKA' Bogie Borail 'Osprey' Wagons, fitted with stanchions, which enable 30ft and 60ft track panels to be secured on the wagons without strapping.   **Neil Harvey**

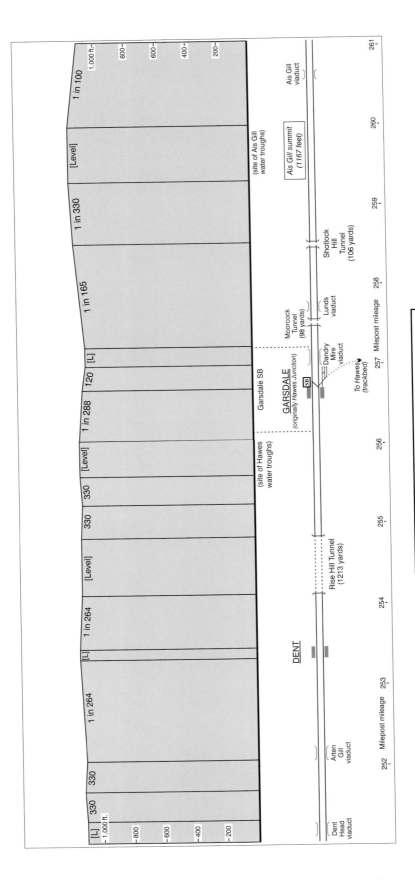

Dent Head - Ais Gill

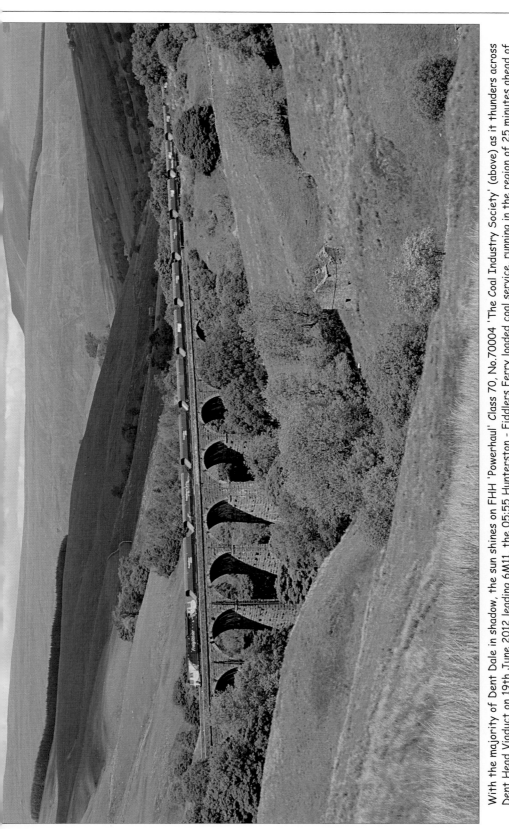

With the majority of Dent Dale in shadow, the sun shines on FHH 'Powerhaul' Class 70, No.70004 'The Coal Industry Society' (above) as it thunders across Dent Head Viaduct on 19th June 2012 leading 6M11, the 05:55 Hunterston - Fiddlers Ferry loaded coal service, running in the region of 25 minutes ahead of schedule. Dent Head Viaduct's vital statistics read: 10 arches, 596ft long, 110 feet high and built of 'blue' limestone.

James Welham

ARTEN GILL VIADUCT

This magnificent viaduct is one of the highest viaducts on the Settle & Carlisle and carries the line over Arten Gill Beck, a post glacial stream which has cut into the valley side. It was built between 1871 - 1874 using massive blocks of 'Dent marble' from the now-disused nearby quarries and its statistics read: 11 arches, 660 feet in length and 117ft high.

Bright sunshine illuminates the spectacular Arten Gill viaduct on 24th September 2008 as an unidentified Northern Class 158 unit (above) heads north on the 14.49hrs Leeds - Carlisle 'stopper'. **John Longden**

(Opposite) : I think my aching calf muscles will always remind me of the trek up the hillside to reach this vantage point, but the view of the viaduct looking towards Dent was well worth the effort. On 25th March 2003, Class 66/0 No.66044 sweeps round over the viaduct with a uniform rake of 2-axle 'HAA' hoppers loaded with coal, running as 6U51, Ayr Falkland Yard - Drax. **Martin Buck**

Viewed from the opposite side of the line on 25th June 1988, InterCity-liveried Class 47/4 No.47593 'Galloway Princess' (below) heads over the viaduct with 1M43, 10:42 Leeds - Carlisle. **Neil Harvey**

DENT

Dent railway station serves the villages of Cowgill and Dent, operated by Northern Rail who provide all passenger train services. Dent village is just under 5-miles away by road and 600ft below the height of the station. At an altitude of 1,150ft, Dent is the highest railway station on the National Rail network in England; the station buildings are now privately owned and during the 1970s they were rented out to Barden school in Burnley as an outdoor pursuits centre.

"You drive all the way from Halifax, hoping the sun will stay out long enough for the required shot, nearly, but not quite". GBRf Class 66/7 No.66708 (above) approaches Dent on 11th July 2006 with 4M91, the 13:16 Cottam - Newbiggin loaded gypsum.   **Neil Harvey**

This is a 'classic' view of Dent station, clearly showing the station buildings and remains of the old snow fences on the hillside above the line. On 21st May 2012, the Network Rail Measurement Train - No.43062 leading & No.43013 rear (below) - passes through the station with 1Q36, Heaton - Derby. **John Longden**

Rise Hill Tunnel

After Dent, the line runs for another three quarters of a mile before reaching Rise Hill Tunnel.

Making a change from the usual FHH Class 66/5 green machines is Class 66/4 No.66425 (above), hired from DRS on 6th May 2008 to work 6M32, the 09:37 Greenburn - Ratcliffe. The train rounds the curve, about to enter Dent station, with the south portal of the tunnel visible in the distance.

Almost two weeks later, the colourful Shanks liveried Class 66/5 No.66522 (below) puts in an appearance and, with the lime green end facing the train, crawls out of the tunnel towards Dent station just ahead of a patch of cloud with 6E73, the 05:50 Hunterston - Drax loaded coal.

If you compare these two images with the one on Page 153, you will see how the conifers have grown since being planted as saplings over 30 years ago.

John Longden (2)

Garsdale Troughs

Spring : Leaving Rise Hill Tunnel behind, the line hugs the hillside with the River Clough down below, reaching a level section of track and the site of the former Garsdale water troughs. The troughs were once used by steam locos to replenish their supply of water and, at 1,670 feet, were the highest in the world.

On 2nd March 2007, 'celebrity' DRS Class 66/4 No.66411 'Eddie the Engine' (above) heads the diverted 'Tesco Express' (4S43, 07:21 Daventry - Mossend), suitably adorned in Stobart Rail colours, with just a few yards to go to reach Garsdale station.   **Richard Armstrong**

Summer : On 17th September 2010, GBRf Class 66/7 No.66701 'Whitemoor' (below), in original 'Bluebird' livery, is seen heading towards Garsdale with 4S51, the 07:45 Drax - Hunterston coal empties.   **Ross Byers**

Autumn : "The early bird catches the worm ...."

In early morning light, the sun just about highlights the autumnal colours as FHH Class 66/5 No.66581 (above) sneaks under the bridge on the approach to the former troughs with 6M38, the 04:30 Earles Sidings - Brunthill cement on 9th November 2007.   **Dave McAlone**

Winter : With deep snow hampering the walk to this location, DBS Class 66/0 No.66114 (below) blasts onto the level from Garsdale with a lightweight 6M00, the 07:00 Mossend - Clitheroe on 4th January 2010. The snow on the hillside gives an indication of how deep the snow was on this particular visit.   **John Longden**

GARSDALE

A Junction Station : Apart from Settle Junction, Garsdale was the only junction on the route where a line diverged through Wensleydale to Hawes and Northallerton on the East Coast Main Line. The Hawes branch sadly closed in 1959, although the trackbed is mostly still intact.

It has been known as Hawes Junction, Hawes Junction & Garsdale, and Garsdale for Hawes. Today, it is simply known as Garsdale, having closed in 1970 and reopened in 1986.

Turntable : In the halcyon days of steam, pilot engines were turned on the stockaded turntable for the return to Hellifield or Carlisle after double-heading heavy freight trains to this point. Apparently, on one windy night in 1900, the wind caught a loco and spun it round for several hours until someone had the idea of pouring sand into the well to bring things to a stop. After that, the turntable was provided with a wind fence of old sleepers. This happening provided the inspiration for the story Tenders and Turntables in the book "Troublesome Engines" in The Railway Series by Rev W. Awdry. The turntable was dismantled and moved in 1990 to a new home on the Keighley & Worth Valley Railway.

Garsdale Signal Box is a Midland Railway type 4c design, fitted with a 40 lever Tappet frame. The 'box opened on 10th July 1910 and replaced the 1892-built Hawes Junction South and the 1891-built Hawes Junction North signal boxes.

The 'Coal Road' is a minor road going over the fells from Garsdale to Dent, providing a quick journey between the two places for travellers (especially useful for railway photographers), rather than taking the 'long way round' via the A684, to Sedburgh.

There were twenty-five coal pits on the moorland either side of the Coal Road, worked by local people to produce domestic fuel but, by the 18th century, the coal was also used in lime kilns. Commercial mining in Garsdale lasted until the 1870s, when the railway started bringing in cheaper (and higher) quality coal from the Lancashire and West Yorkshire coalfields.

A Sad Tale : *On the northern end of the 'Up' platform, there is a bronze statue commemorating a dog called 'Ruswarp', the faithful companion of Graham Nuttall, one of the two founders of the FOSCL.*

'Ruswarp' made headlines in the 1980s, placing a paw print on a petition to resist closure. Less than a year after the 'S & C' was reprieved, Graham and 'Ruswarp' went walking in the Welsh hills on 20th January 1990, never to return. Nearly eleven weeks later, Graham's body was found and 'Ruswarp' lay nearby, keeping vigil over his master. Although nursed back to health, he lived long enough to attend Graham's funeral and a bench on the 'Down' platform commemorates Graham Nuttall with 'Ruswarp' gazing towards the bench.

Garsdale Station

Looking north east (above), an unidentified Class 158 unit is approaching the station on 20th January 2011 with the 14:00hrs Carlisle - Leeds service, eagerly awaited by three passengers.   **Dave McAlone**

Garsdale Signal Box (opposite) was 'switched out' for long periods from 1983 when British Rail deliberately decided to run down the line but, by the start of 1987, the 'box was opened on an 'as required' basis, usually for weekend WCML diversions. From 2004, Garsdale signal box was refurbished and opened for 24 hours a day due to increased traffic volumes.

Looking south west (below) across the 'Up Refuge Sidings' and main running lines towards the quaint little station, the 'S & C' looks to be still in the grip of winter; the date is 9th April 1994. To the left of the sidings is the trackbed of the former six mile branch line to Hawes, where it made an end-on junction with the North Eastern Railway (NER) line from Northallerton.   **Keith McGovern (2)**

Garsdale Head

A different take on a southbound coal train .... viewed from the A684 Sedburgh to Hawes road on a freezing 13th December 2012, DBS Class 66/0 No.66164 (above) is glimpsed shortly after leaving Moorcock Tunnel, above the A684 road, approaching Garsdale with another trainload of the black stuff. **John Longden**

What a cracker .... FHH 'celebrity' loco, Class 66/6 No.66623 'Bill Bolsover' (below), sweeps round the curve off Dandry Mire Viaduct on 24th March 2011, picking

up at gain to an iron a lane ad the ash Garsdale station with 6573 the 05:50 Uustonston West Burton coal.

Neil Harvey

Dandry Mire Viaduct

Looking every inch the model railway, Colas Rail Class 56s, Nos.56087 + 56105 (above), clatter over the 12-arch Dandry Mire Viaduct on 11th July 2013, approaching Garsdale leading 6J37, the 10:37 Carlisle Yard – Chirk timber. This service needs a pair of 'grids' as the route is too arduous for a single Class 56 to cope with a

A "Brief Encounter" on 17th September 2010 as two freight trains are about to pass one another on Dandry Mire Viaduct. GBRf Class 66/7 No.66708 'Jayne' (above) heads north over the viaduct with 4S51, the 07:45 Drax - Hunterston coal empties and meets DBS Class 66/0 No.66108 on 6M00, the 07:03 Mossend - Clitheroe cement empties. An embankment was originally planned here but, after tipping $\frac{3}{4}$ million cubic feet of earth which just kept sinking into the bog, it was decided a viaduct would be a better idea. Built between 1871 and 1872, Dandry Mire (Moorcock) Viaduct has 12 arches, is 50 feet high and 227 yards long.   **John Longden**

Lunds

In stunning evening Spring light, GBRf's 'Metronet' Class 66/7 No.66722 'Sir Edward Watkin' (above) has exited the 98-yard long Moorcock Tunnel and powers across the five-arch Lunds Viaduct, climbing towards Ais Gill on 27th April 2011 with 4C77, Fiddler's Ferry - Newbiggin loaded gypsum.　　**John Longden**

On 2nd November 2011, the DBS Management Train (below), consisting of Class 82 DVT No.82146 + three Mk3 coaches + Class 67 No.67029 'Royal Diamond' is seen approaching Grisedale on the outward journey of a circular trip to and from York. The plate-girder footbridge in view was built in 1936 to replace an 1886 wooden structure, it is the only one of its type on the line.　　**James Welham**

Shotlock Hill

The iconic 2-axle 'HAA' MGR coal hopper just has something about it, perhaps character, which latter day bogie coal hoppers don't seem to have. On 5th May 2007, EWS Class 66/0 No.66167 (above) hauls a rake of these hoppers and is seen approaching Shotlock Tunnel with 6Z74, the 10:13 New Cumnock - Ratcliffe.

The main B6259 road which goes over Shotlock Hill from Moorcock shadows the line via Ais Gill and Mallerstang, then through the Eden Valley to Nateby (near Kirkby Stephen), as we can see here. On 5th May 2007, EWS 'Beasties' adorned Class 60 No.60063 'James Murray' (below) leaves Shotlock Tunnel with 6M52, the 09:36 Drax - Newbiggin loaded gypsum, with just a mile to go to the summit at Ais Gill. **Neil Harvey (2)**

Lunds

In the late 1980s / early 1990s, the daily loco-hauled services between Leeds and Carlisle were usually powered by either Class 31/4 or Class 47/4 locos, both Classes fitted with Electric Train Heating (ETH) to provide warmth for the passengers onboard. On 14th July 1990, Class 31/4 No.31410 (left) passes Lunds in fine style with 1E11, the 12:43 Carlisle to Leeds.

The northern skyline is broken by the unmistakable Millstone Grit capped flat top of Wild Boar Fell, which looms 2,324 feet high. **Neil Harvey**

Shaw Paddock

FHH Class 66/5 No.66551 (below) powers through Shaw Paddock, having passed through Shotlock Hill tunnel, on 23rd June 2008 with used ballast from an engineer's possession at Clitheroe (Horrocksford Junction), heading for the discharge point at Carlisle Yard.

The actual tunnel through Shotlock Hill is a mere 108 yards long and, in view of the local topography, would a cutting have been a more cost effective proposition? **John Longden**

AIS GILL

The summit of the line at 1,169 feet above sea level is the highest point on a main line in England but, alas, nothing remains here today, save for a summit board. There used to be ....

Refuge Sidings were once situated here, which had no 'facing points' into the sidings, only 'trailing points'. This meant that slow good trains had to pass the siding first before setting back into them and then await a path in order to proceed on their journey!

Ais Gill Signal Box opened on 6th April 1890, but closed on 28th January 1981.

For several years after closing, like at many other locations, the semaphore signals here remained in situ but set permanently to the 'off' position. In this instance, this became an extremely long 'block' section of 17 miles between Kirkby Stephen and Blea Moor, which could cause a bottleneck. However, Garsdale 'box could be opened when necessary to help alleviate delays.

Fortunately, Ais Gill Signal Box was saved and is preserved at the Midland Railway Centre, Butterley, Derbyshire.

Gradient Profile : From Settle, the line climbs for some 15 miles at a ruling gradient of 1 in 100 until Blea Moor Tunnel. From here, the line effectively runs 'level' until Garsdale, after which there's a further three miles of 1 in 165 / 1 in 330 before the summit is reached.

Southbound, there's a steady climb of 15 miles at 1 in 100 from Ormside, which means the climb to Ais Gill summit is equally as gruelling in both directions.

AIS GILL SUMMIT

Nearly there .... Transrail Class 60 No.60015 'Bowfell' (above) starts to level off, having made the climb to the summit on 14th February 1998 with a southbound loaded MGR service. The destination is Drax power station and the train is either the 08:47hrs (7Z38) or 10:38hrs (7Z39) departure from Hunterston Import terminal.

Neil Harvey

AIS GILL SUMMIT

(Left) : This is the 'old' Midland Railway Summit board, located at 259 miles and 57 chains, on the 'Down' side of the main line, showing an elevation of 1,169ft above sea level. The date is June 1980.   **Martin Buck**

(Below) : At just after half-past-two in the afternoon of 10th March 2010, Class 66/0 No.66084 (below) breasts the summit with 4E13, the 12:40 Newbiggin - Doncaster Decoy Yard empty gypsum. Note the 'new' summit board to the right of the loco on the 'Up' side of the line.   **John Longden**

Seasonal variations

The weather can be changeable and unpredictable, one aspect of the 'S & C' of which every rambler and railway photographer is all too aware, but when the sun shines the rewards are great ....

Arctic Blue! Even more snow, than already on the ground, fell overnight to give the deepest snow conditions for over a decade. Photographing on 6th January 2010 was real 'Boys Own' adventure stuff, by following a snow plough up to Ais Gill and wading through waist deep snow in places to get to this location. The wind was howling and snow drifted very quickly, any water would freeze on the face instantly - Kirkby Stephen weather station reported a windchill of -7 degrees!

In superb, but freezing, conditions, FHH Class 66/6 No.66623 'Bill Bolsover' (top right) crawls past Ais Gill with a special 6Z73, Killoch - Ratcliffe loaded coal service.   **John Longden**

Spring Greens : FHH Class 66/5 No.66520 + 'Powerhaul' Class 70 No.70004 DIT (bottom right) slogs past Milepost 260 on the last stretch of the climb to the summit at Ais Gill on 28th May 2012, while working 6Z68, the 07:22 Killoch - Drax loaded coal hoppers - impressive!   **Steven Brykajlo**

ACCIDENTS AT THE SUMMIT

January 1995

A rail accident occurred near Ais Gill at about 18:55hrs on 31st January 1995. A Class 156 Super-Sprinter was derailed by a landslide and was subsequently run into by a similar train travelling in the opposite direction. Sadly, the conductor of the first train, Mr Stuart Wilson, was fatally injured in the collision.

Events :

A Class 156 Super-Sprinter forming 2H88, the 16:26 Carlisle - Leeds only got as far Ribblehead railway station, as the lines from Ribblehead to Settle were blocked by flooding, and had to return to Carlisle. The driver changed cabs and headed northbound instead of southbound, back over Ribblehead Viaduct, and on to Ais Gill Summit; it was dark and raining heavily.

Near Ais Gill Summit, the train hit a landslide and derailed across both tracks. The injured driver managed to make an emergency call to 'Control', but this could not prevent the subsequent collision. The conductor escorted passengers into the rear unit, which was across the northbound track, returning to see the driver who was still in the cab. The front lights of the stricken unit were changed from white to red to warn oncoming trains of the obstruction.

Meanwhile, the Super-Sprinter forming 2H92, the 17:45 Carlisle - Leeds had set off from Kirkby Stephen and about a quarter of a mile before the derailed train, the driver saw its red lights and applied an emergency brake application. Unfortunately, the conductor of the derailed train was killed and 30 passengers on both trains were injured.

September 1913

This accident occurred on 2nd September 1913 and the cause of the crash was a signal passed at danger (known as a 'SPAD', nowadays!), although there were other contributing factors.

Events :

The two trains involved were both passenger, having left Carlisle in the early hours of 2nd September 1913 bound for London St. Pancras.

At the time, the Midland Railway had a policy of using 'small' steam locos, which had barely sufficient power to tackle the gradients on the line working the heavy trains. Apparently, the first loco's load was 13 tons over its maximum limit (230 tons) and the driver asked for a pilot engine, but to no avail. To make matters worse, both steam locos were using coal that was full of slack and 'small coal' which would not fire well.

The first train left Carlisle at 01:38hrs and, struggling up to Ais Gill summit, the steam pressure on the loco steadily dropped until the train stalled half a mile short of the summit. As they cleaned out the grate and tried to build up steam pressure, the driver and fireman erroneously told the guard they would only be standing for a few minutes. As a result, the guard did not protect the rear of the train by laying detonators or walking back along the line with a lantern.

Meanwhile, the second train was also struggling and just short of Mallerstang the driver left the cab to walk round the outside framing and oil some of the working parts, while the train was in motion. At the same time, the fireman was having difficulty getting an injector to work and the boiler water level was dropping. When the driver returned, both men worked on the injector and eventually restarted it. Distracted by their work, they missed all the Mallerstang signals, a red lantern being waved by the Mallerstang signalman and another being waved by the guard of the first train. Shortly after, they looked up, but it was too late.

The second train demolished a rear parcels van and ploughed into a third-class coach. The roof of the parcels van slid over the second engine and sliced into a first class sleeping car. Flammable gas from the cylinders for the gas-oil lighting system ignited and spread a fire. Fourteen people in the first train died at the scene and two more passengers subsequently died of their injuries. Thirty-eight passengers in the second train were seriously injured.

West Coast Diversions

It seems rather incredulous that British Rail would even consider closing a route which has such strategic importance when it comes to diversionary train planning, especially so when the West Coast Main Line is closed! By way of example:

In the 1970s, the Settle & Carlisle came into its own as a diversionary route when Anglo-Scottish expresses between Preston and Carlisle were diverted during weekends, to facilitate the electrification of the WCML. This practice minimised disruption to train schedules and any inconvenience to passengers but, following full electrification in 1974, diversions became less frequent.

During 1979, some East Coast Main Line freight services were also diverted over the 'S & C' to ease congestion on the ECML due to the Penmanshiel Tunnel collapse.

Even in March 1989, two months before closure was averted, there were wholesale passenger diversions for several weekends, so essential engineering work could be carried out on the WCML. This practice continued into the '90s and enthusiasts could enjoy a procession of expresses hauled by Class 47s, sporting a variety of liveries, as we will see.

Nowadays, with the advent of Voyager units and Pendolino EMUs 'dragged' by a Class 57/3 loco, it's not quite the same - so, let's reminisce ....

BR Parcels sector Class 47/4 No.47476 'Night Mail' (above) sporting dark grey and red colours approaches Ais Gill Summit on 30th March 1993 with a northbound west coast diversion. The train is formed of InterCity liveried Mk2f air-conditioned coaches plus 'BG' brake van.

(Previous Page): **Network South East** Class 47/4 No.47587 is a rare visitor to the 'S & C', seen crossing Arten Gill Viaduct with a southbound diversion on 27th March 1993. This blue, white and red livery, came into being in 1986, when 'London & South Eastern' passenger sector became Network South East (NSE).

Civil Engineer 'Dutch' Grey / Yellow ex-Class 47/4 No.47976 'Aviemore Centre' (below) heads a diverted express over Dandry Mire Viaduct on 27th March 1993. This '47' was named 'Aviemore Centre' in May 1985, renumbered from No.47546 in June 1990 and cut up at Wigan in April 2000.

Railfreight Grey, Large Logo Class 47/3 No.47365 'Diamond Jubilee' (above) is in charge of the 12:37hrs Glasgow Central - London Euston on 11th March 1989 and is passing Blea Moor; chilly, no doubt, with a 'no heat' Class 47 on the front! No.47340 is stabled alongside the signal box as stand-by cover. No.47365 was named 'Diamond Jubilee' at ICI Wilton on 20th September 1986.

LNER-style Apple Green was a unique livery applied to Class 47/4 No.47522 in conjunction with it being named 'Doncaster Enterprise' on 3rd October 1987 by Councillor Gladys Ambler, Mayor of Doncaster, at Doncaster Works open day. Here, No.47522 (below) approaches a slightly misty Horton-in-Ribblesdale on 30th April 1988 with a northbound WCML diversion. **Neil Harvey (5)**

Class 31s : Quite a surprise is in store for enthusiasts waiting to see the diverted 09:08hrs Glasgow Central - Brighton on 18th March 1989 as, when the train enters Long Preston, there are 2 x Class 31s, No.31292 and No.31413 'Severn Valley Railway' (above) on the front. Class 31s were very unusual on Settle & Carlisle diversions - hence the inclusion of this shot, taken in typical 'S & C' weather!

No.31413's livery looked more like a patchwork quilt with a strange mix of BR Blue, grey roof, plus a strange looking pale blue lower body stripe and lower red stripe wrapped round the cab bottom!

Class 37 : Another rarity; a Class 37 working a diverted west coast express but, by the time word got out, there was only time for a quick dash to the Hellifield - Blackburn line to record the event. On 2nd May 1987, Thornaby-based Class 37/0 No.37135 (below) is seen heading 1E87, the 10:15 Glasgow Central - Harwich, as it passes Newsholme (between Hellifield and Gisburn).

No.37135 was one of the Class 37s transferred to Spain for infrastructure work in May 2004, before being withdrawn in February 2007 and cut up in Puig Vert in July the same year.   **Neil Harvey (2)**

60094

BR **Trainload Construction** Class 60 No.60094 'Tryfan' (above) pilots InterCity Class 47 No.47973 'Derby Evening Post' with the diverted 1S57, 10:15hrs London Euston - Glasgow Central 'Royal Scot' on Saturday, 24th April 1993. The 'tug' is passing Ais Gill, having already worked south (see below). The loco carries dark blue and yellow chequered Construction sector decals; other sector decals were Black & Yellow (Coal), Yellow & Red (Railfreight Distribution), Red & Yellow (Railfreight International), Yellow & Blue Chevrons (Metals), Yellow & Blue Waves (Petroleum).

Neil Harvey

Earlier in the day, No.60094 (below) was captured approaching Blea Moor signal box with the diverted 09:24 Edinburgh Waverley - Birmingham New Street. Operationally, the Class 60 is well suited, being a 60mph loco working on a 60mph railway!

Keith McGovern

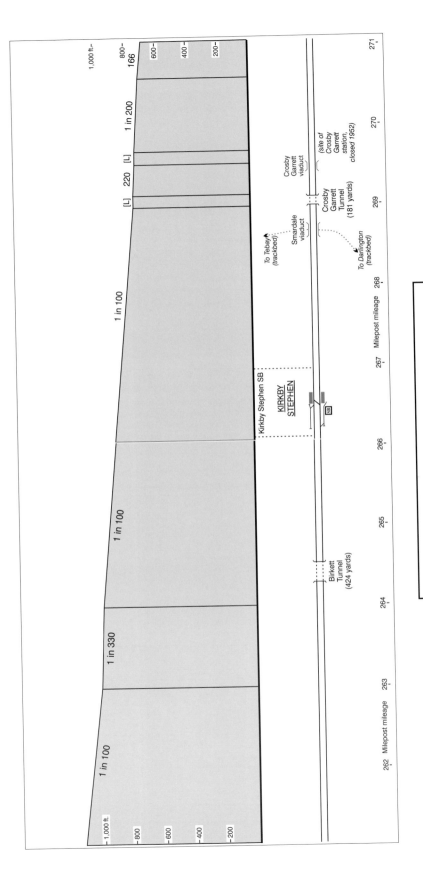

Ais Gill - Crosby Garrett

Crosby Garrett : It's just before 07:00hrs as DB Schenker Class 66/0 No.66176 (above) is recorded thundering high over a sleepy Crosby Garrett village whilst leading 6Z88, the 03:43 Doncaster Belmont - Carlisle Yard empty 'MEA' box wagons.   **James Welham**

Mallerstang

The Area : Mallerstang is in the east of Cumbria, at the head of the upper Eden Valley, originally part of Westmorland. It is bounded by Wild Boar Fell and Swarth Fell to the west and Mallerstang Edge to the east. The highest point of Mallerstang Edge is High Seat (2,326ft above sea level) and about three feet higher than the more prominent Wild Boar Fell.

The other main high points on the eastern side of the dale are the curiously named Gregory Chapel, south of High Seat, and Hugh Seat to the south-east.

The River Eden rises as Red Gill Beck in the peat bogs of Black Moss, below Hugh Seat. A little further downstream it becomes Hellgill Beck, taking the name 'Eden' below Hell Gill Force waterfall, after it is joined by Aisgill Beck, which flows down from Wild Boar Fell. The River Eden ultimately empties into the sea at the Solway Firth, near Carlisle.

About a quarter of a mile before the railway reaches Birkett Tunnel, there are the ruins of Pendragon Castle in the valley below, which is the legendary seat of King Arthur's father, Uther Pendragon. The castle was burnt down by the Scots in 1541 and rebuilt by Lady Anne Clifford in 1660.

The Railway : After crossing Ais Gill viaduct, the line clings to the side of Wild Boar Fell for about four miles until reaching the south portal of Birkett Tunnel. This really is a delightful part of the journey for rail passengers, espying the magnificent Pennine scenery through the carriage window.

The view looking up to the railway from the B6259 road in the valley below is equally breathtaking, with passing trains almost 'model-like' in appearance, clinging to the hillside.

Mallerstang Common : This is the view looking northwards up the valley with the rugged outcrop of Mallerstang Edge dominating the background; the line curves round the base of Wild Boar Fell through Angerholme and onwards towards Birkett Tunnel and Kirkby Stephen.

With the remnants of yesterday's heavy snow fall melting away, No.70006 (above) crosses Ais Gill viaduct on 5th April 2012 with a regular loaded coal working, 6M32, the 10:03 Killoch - Ratcliffe; the diagram on which the Class 70 first started to appear after their arrival in the UK.　**John Longden**

Angerholme

Whilst waiting to press the shutter for the normal shot at Angerholme, Milepost 261, (once the loco has passed under the overbridge) this earlier shot shows FHH Class 66/5 No.66553 (top right) nicely framed by the red brick structure.

The old decrepit fences either side balance the shot whilst the huge flank of Mallerstang Edge looms large in the background. The date is 29th May 2012 and the train is 6M32, the 10:03 Killoch - Ratcliffe. **John Longden**

Meanwhile, on 9th January 2012, Northern Rail Class 158 unit No.158872 (middle) is seen also heading south with the 15:05 Carlisle - Leeds. This view clearly shows the height of the line above the valley below.   **Ian Ball**

A long wait at Angerholme is rewarded on 3rd February 2009 with the arrival of FHH low-emission Class 66/9 No.66951 (below), which is seen here working through a beautiful snowy scene with 6Z73, the 04:47 Killoch - Ratcliffe. **John Longden**

Birkett Common

On 14th April 2007, EWS Class 66/0 No.66013 (above) sweeps into Birkett Common, after leaving Birkett Tunnel, with 6S55, the diverted 22:26 (Fri) Burngullow - Irvine loaded china clay. During winter and early spring, it is commonplace for weekend Virgin West Coast passenger, along with some freight services, to be diverted via the 'S & C', due to scheduled engineering work on the WCML.

On 9th August 2006, a 4Z10, Carlisle - Skipton test train brightens things up on the Common. Heart of Wessex Line promotional liveried (cerise pink) Class 31/6 No.31601 'The Mayor of Casterbridge' (below) heads south, top 'n' tailed with an unidentified sister loco bringing up the rear.   **Richard Armstrong (2)**

Low Frith : This location is at the north end of Mallerstang and was very popular during the last days of steam but seems rarely visited in modern times. It's probably at its best in November when the collection of silver birch trees are on the turn. With the golden brown trees lining the line, Class 60 No.60028 'John Flamsteed' (above) powers past on 3rd November 2006 in charge of 6E13, the 12:40 Newbiggin - Milford.

Bull Gill : On the first weekend of WCML diversions in 2011, 2 x 'Super Voyagers' No.221107 + No.221115 (below) climb quickly through Bull Gill in clear spring light with the diverted Virgin West Coast 1M91, 12:52 Edinburgh Waverley - Birmingham New Street.

John Longden (2)

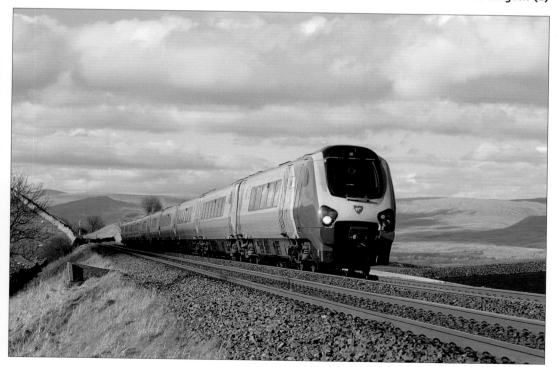

Birkett Common : At last, S & C logs! It's been a long time coming, but today (12th March 2010) is the first routing of 6J37, the 12:44 Carlisle Yard – Chirk logs via the Settle & Carlisle. The usual traction is a Colas liveried Class 66/8 and the colourful No.66843 (above) is seen climbing slowly through Birkett Common with its load of Kielder Forest timber. From January 2011, the payload increases to 21 'KFAs'.

John Longden

Waitby : As with the previous image, another stunning composition to show off the beautiful scenery associated with the Settle & Carlisle; the distant fells, dry-stone walls, animals grazing in the pastures and a train - what more could one want? On 26th May 2007, Class 66/0 No.66098 (above) heads north at Waitby with 6S67, the 11:26 Milford Sidings - Chalmerston empty 'HTA' coal hoppers, returning to Ayrshire to be loaded with yet more of the black stuff.   **Neil Harvey**

(Left) : On 9th June 2011, DBS Class 66/0, No.66112 passes Kirkby Stephen Signalbox leading 6S00, the 17:05 Clitheroe - Mossend Down Yard loaded cement tanks.

The signal box, which replaced the original 'box a few yards further south, looks out of place compared with other structures on the line. The former goods shed is also in view, which closed to freight traffic in September 1964. **James Welham**

(Below) : If you look at the quaint posting box and telephone box, you could be forgiven in thinking this is a model railway, but no ....

.... in glorious sunshine, Class 66/0 No.66144 enters Kirkby Stephen station on 9th June 2007 with 6M80, the 10:10 New Cumnock - Toton loaded 'HTA' coal hoppers.

The 'HTAs' were introduced by EWS from 2001 for use on MGR coal trains, capable of carrying 75 tonnes and running at 60mph loaded. These wagons replaced the 'HAA' 2-axle hoppers built in the 1960s. **Dave McAlone**

KIRKBY STEPHEN

The Station lies about two miles to the west of the town, just south of the busy main road from Kendal to Brough, located here due to the railway line needing a suitable elevation for the climb to Ais Gill.

It closed in May 1970, but reopened in July 1986.

The North Eastern Railway also had a station in the town - Kirkby Stephen East - which opened in 1861 and closed in 1962, situated on the west side of the A685 road. It was originally on the South Durham & Lancashire Union Railway linking Barnard Castle and Tebay.

Built in 1875, to the same specification as Appleby and Settle, Kirkby Stephen had the distinction of being the only station on the 'S & C' to have the luxury of a first class waiting room.

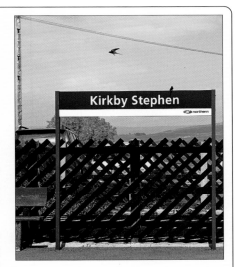

Names : The present day station has had several names in its history:

1875 : Kirkby Stephen	1900 : Kirkby Stephen and Ravenstonedale
1935 : Kirkby Stephen	1953 : Kirkby Stephen West *
1968 : Kirkby Stephen	

* to differentiate from the North Eastern station.

Signal Box : The present day structure is a British Railways London Midland Region Type 15 design, fitted with a 20 lever London Midland Region Standard frame, opening in October 1974. This one replaced the 1894-built Midland Railway Type 2a design signal box, using parts from Kendal signal box, which closed in April 1973.

(Above) : The finely restored Midland Railway station at Kirkby Stephen.

(Inset) : Does more than one Swallow make a summer?

James Welham
Dave McAlone

Smardale

On 23rd April 1988, Class 47/4 No.47523 (above) is seen heading 1M43, the 10:40 York - Carlisle, passing Smardale, in a clearing between two cuttings. The lane leading up to the line links Waitby and Smardale.

This service also originated from Hull during the previous two years but, mostly in the early 1990s until loco-hauled trains finished, these services settled down to run between Leeds and Carlisle.   **Neil Harvey**

6K05

12:18, Carlisle Yard - Crewe Basford Hall

This is the only timetabled departmental (engineer's) service to run over the Settle & Carlisle and is the return working of the morning 6C02, Crewe Basford Hall - Carlisle Yard. The train can be an interesting proposition for both enthusiasts and photographers as it can have a mix of wagons and can also include other locos 'DIT' (Dead in Transit), which are being repositioned to eliminate light engine moves.

From August 2013, the responsibility of providing motive power for this service transfers from DB Schenker (DBS) to Direct Rail Services (DRS) .....

(Opposite)

DBS provided the loco for 6K05 from 2009. On 8th March 2010, Network Rail points carriers are part of the formation, which accounts for an 'out of gauge' reporting code of 6X05 on this occasion. The train is seen here cruising across Waitby Common behind Class 66/0 No. 66192 (top right) with the 12:18hrs service from Carlisle Yard to Crewe Basford Hall.   **John Longden**

DRS are now the new order and diagram a Class 66/4 loco for 6C02/6K05, although DRS 37s can sometimes substitute. On 7th August 2013, No.66431 (bottom right) climbs through Smardale with 6K05, formed of a long rake of 2-axle Open Wagons, coded 'MFA', 'MHA' and 'MTA'.   **Neil Harvey**

(Overleaf)

Smardale Viaduct : On 2nd May 2007, the timetable was in chaos because this passenger working was running at least 2 hours late due to a unit failure, which accounts for a Class 142 'Pacer' unit being pressed into action over the 'S & C'! No.142079 (page 82), heads over Smardale Viaduct, the photographer enjoying the view from the hillside and is probably a lot more comfortable than on the seats aboard the crowded unit.

Smardale Cutting : A complete contrast, FHH Class 66/5 No.66512 ((page 83)) heads 6M11, the 04:38, Killoch - Fiddlers Ferry loaded coal hoppers on 3rd April 2013 through Smardale Cutting. The loco is working hard on the climb south through the deep rock cutting, framed by the brick overbridge, on a deceptively cold day and the attractive scene doesn't give any indication of the wind chill.   **John Longden (2)**

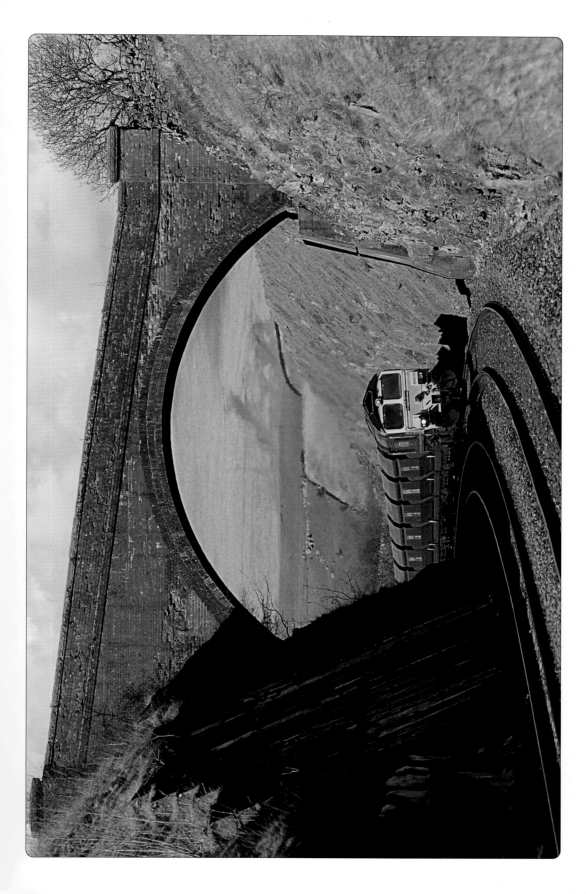

Waitby Common

Ah, the good old days of loco-hauled travel, sitting comfortably in a Mk1 compartment or open stock seat. On 25th June 1988, just under a year before the 'S & C' is saved from closure, Class 47/5 No.47595 'Confederation of British Industry' (above) climbs past Waitby with 1E33, the 16:15 Carlisle - Leeds.

A super composition, the unit is almost secondary in the beautiful Pennine landscape. On 23rd April 1988, an unidentified Class 108 Diesel Multiple Unit (below) is seen at Waitby with 1M43, the 11:06 Leeds - Carlisle, at a time when the local stopping trains were in the hands of these first-generation units. **Neil Harvey (2)**

With a 33-minute early departure from Clitheroe on 28th September 2011, there was just a slight chance that the loaded cement tanks would arrive in the upper Eden Valley before sun down. With just minutes to spare, Class 66/0 No.66075 (above) rolls onto the embankment at Waitby Common in stunning golden light with 6S00, the 17:05 Clitheroe - Mossend. **John Longden**

Here, on 9th January 2012, we see one of the infrequent stone trains from Shap to Leeds passing Waitby with a good selection of bogie hoppers: ex-RMC 'JGAs', ex-EWS and ex-Cemex branded 'HOAs' and some 'IIAs'. Class 66/0 No.66099 (below) passes Waitby with 6Z56, Shap - Leeds Stourton. **Ian Ball**

Crosby Garrett

The Midland Railway station at Crosby Garrett opened in 1876 and was closed by British Rail in 1952 as an economy measure.

The platforms were set into the cutting, needing hefty retaining walls and, whilst overgrown, they have partly survived to this day.

Before the station, the line plunges into Crosby Garrett Tunnel (181 yards long) and then over the viaduct, which is 110 yards long, 55 feet high with six arches.

On 15th January 1999, 10-minutes shy of eight o'clock in the evening, the 17:12hrs Huddersfield - Carlisle Northern Spirit passenger train collided with a landslip at Crosby Garrett Tunnel and derails, blocking the adjacent line. The driver is able to warn an oncoming EWS coal train of the danger by using a warning light and placing detonators on the track.

The driver of the coal train slows, but is unable to prevent it running into the derailed passenger train, which was pushed back around 90 metres into the tunnel. The train crew required hospital treatment and, fortunately, no passengers were injured.

Tunnel : On 20th December 2007, No.66425 (top) leaves the south portal of Crosby Garrett Tunnel with 6E36, Killoch - West Burton loaded coal. This came as a complete surprise as this train was not expected to run and, when it does, turns up with a hired-in DRS Class 66/4 loco.   **John Longden**

Viaduct : A panoramic view looking towards the distant Pennine Fells illustrates Crosby Garrett Viaduct and its six arches. On 4th May 2011, FHH Class 66/6 No.66615 (above) sweeps across the field of view with 6Z32, the 10:03 Killoch - Ratcliffe loaded coal.   **Neil Harvey**

Station : On 30th October 2003, Class 37/4 No.37408 'Loch Rannoch' (above) passes some fine autumn foliage at Crosby Garrett, as it works 1E23, the 13:33 Carlisle - Leeds Arriva Trains Northern service. No.37411 is bringing up the rear. Note the remains of the old loading dock on the right.   **Martin Loader**

Soulby Road Bridge : On a glorious Spring morning, 8th April 2011, the first Class 66/0 to carry DBS house colours, No.66152 (below) is seen to the north of Crosby Garrett, passing under Soulby Road Bridge, running bang on time with 6M00, the 07:05 Mossend - Clitheroe.   **John Longden**

Griseburn : Class 60 No.60066 'John Logie Baird' (above) is seen leaving an engineer's possession at Griseburn with empty ballast and loaded spoil, running as 6L09, Appleby - Carlisle Yard. The consist is Network Rail 'MRA' Bogie Side Tipping Ballast Wagons (Number range 501001 to 501400) and the yellow coloured wagons are numbered from No.501301 onwards.

Waitby Common : No.60029 'Clitheroe Castle' (top right) waits patiently to enter the possession with 6L12, Appleby - Carlisle Yard loaded ballast. As can be seen, a mechanical digger is involved in work to stabilise the side of the cutting. Meanwhile, at ....

Kirkby Stephen : EWS-liveried No.60030 (bottom right) is seen standing with 6L12, Appleby - Carlisle Yard ballast alongside a 'ZWA' tamping machine stabled in the ex-cattle dock siding. This 60 is at the head of an engineering cavalcade, stretching from Kirkby Stephen to Smardale and consisting of seven members of this class, including (middle image) No.60038 'AvestaPolarit'.

Crosby Garrett : No.60060 'James Watt' (below) heads 6L09, the Appleby - Carlisle Yard 'slinger' train. The 'YFA'-coded 'slinger' wagons form a Jarvis Sleeper Delivery Train (number range 92519 - 92561), built between 1987 - 1988 by Arbel Fauvet, France, and converted between 2001 - 2004 by Jarvis, York. A 'jib' on the 'slinger' lifts new sleepers directly on to freshly laid ballast.

'S & C'
Engineering Work

There are times when Network Rail temporarily close the line, so that essential engineering work can be carried out.

Such work includes replacing worn out track and stabilising cuttings / embankments to prevent landslips.

This involves running trains to a site, bringing in materials (eg. rails, sleepers, ballast, etc), and to take away the old ballast and spoil afterwards.

Class 60s are ideal locos for these trains, as they can operate at slow speed.

In 2007, the Settle & Carlisle was blocked every Saturday and Sunday from July until December. During this time, passenger services were cancelled and any scheduled freight traffic was diverted via Hexham and the ECML.

Five images illustrate some of the trains and the type of work which was being undertaken on 9th July 2007. **Ian Ball (5)**

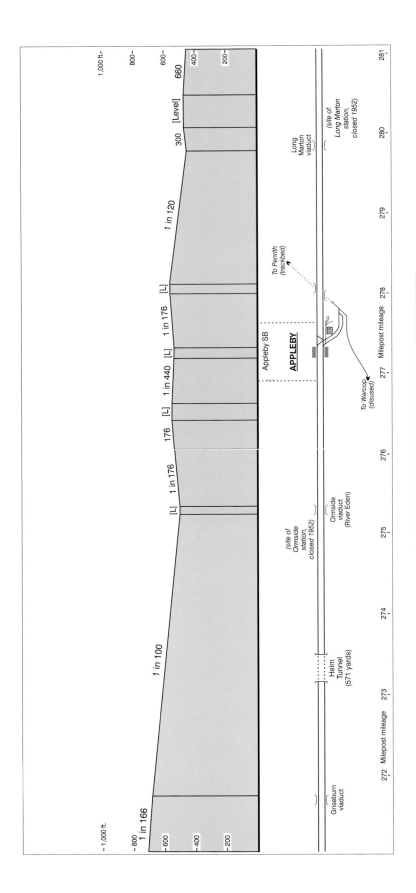

Crosby Garrett - Newbiggin

Keld : On a bright autumnal evening (7th October 2011), Class 57s No.57004 and No.57010 (above) top 'n' tail 3J11, Carlisle - Carlisle RHTT (Railhead Treatment Train) near Town End Farm, north of Keld. Even after operating for a short period of time it's surprising how filthy the rear loco already looks. **John Longden**

Griseburn

After crossing Griseburn Viaduct (7 arches, 74ft high and 142 yards long), the line passes the site of Griseburn ballast sidings, where nearby quarrying took place on behalf of the Midland Railway, becoming disused in 1970. There also used to be a Midland Railway Type 2b design signal box situated on the 'Up' side of the line, just north of Griseburn Viaduct between Ormside and Crosby Garrett.

The signal box opened on 10th October 1905, fitted with a 12 lever Midland Railway Tumbler frame, which replaced an earlier box. It closed on 28th January 1981 when the 'Absolute Block Section' was extended between Appleby North and Kirkby Stephen signal boxes.

The views of Mallerstang edge from this spot at Griseburn are quite attractive and certainly a possible option for shots of northbound services during the afternoon in Spring.

Here we see Northern Rail Class 156 'Sprinter' No.156443 (left), coasting along on 3rd May 2006 with the 14:49 Leeds - Carlisle passenger service.

This colourful livery has since been superceded by deep blue, lilac and white colours.

It had been wall to wall sunshine on this fine autumn day and with the prospect of getting one last shot in decent light. With just seconds to spare before the sun dips behind the hills, DRS Class 66/4s No.66420 and No.66424 (above) come into view heading north on the embankment at Griseburn, top 'n' tailing the 3J06, Carlisle - Carlisle RHTT diagram on 23rd October 2007.   **John Longden (2)**

Ormside

What a beauty .... snow capped Pennine Fells on a crisp and bright early winter's day. Very quiet on the 'S & C' with little running, save for the reliable early afternoon engineer's train. On 13th December 2012, Class 66/0 No.66114 (above) starts out on the real slog to Ais Gill Summit with 6K05, the 12:18 Carlisle Yard - Crewe Basford Hall on 13th December 2012, just another 14-miles of climbing to go!

Appleby (Causey Brow)

During the Summer, Statesman Rail run an 'out & back' steam special on a Wednesday over the 'S & C' from Lancaster to Carlisle, called 'The Fellsman'. Waiting on 27th July 2011 for a volcanic explosion of sound to herald the approach of the 'Fellsman' after leaving Appleby, it's bad news! Apparently, firebox problems at Carlisle meant that the 'Scot' was loco-hauled on the return journey. Snow plough-fitted WCRC Class 47 No.47760 (below), hauls LMS Royal Scot Class 4-6-0 No.46115 'Scots Gaurdsman' away from Appleby, passing Causey Brow with 1Z49, the 15:12 Carlisle - Lancaster.   **John Longden (2)**

APPLEBY

Appleby railway station serves the town of Appleby-in-Westmorland in Cumbria, operated by Northern Rail, who provide all passenger train services. The station was formerly called Appleby West, the older Appleby East station being nearby on the Eden Valley Railway, which served trains on the Darlington - Penrith trans-pennine route. With the closure of the North Eastern Railway (NER) in 1962, the original name of Appleby was reinstated.

Well known railway photographer and enthusiast Bishop Eric Treacy died at Appleby railway station on 13th May 1978 after suffering a heart attack, whilst waiting to photograph BR Class 9f 2-10-0 steam engine No.92220 'Evening Star', which was due to pass through the station on a rail tour. A commemoration plaque is located on the 'down' platform in his memory.

The main brick-built station building, complete with booking office and waiting room, is located on the northbound platform and a period footbridge links the two platforms. There is a water tower at the south end of the platform, which is still used to supply steam engines.

The station opened at the same time as the Settle & Carlisle line by the Midland Railway in May 1876, becoming part of the London, Midland and Scottish Railway in 1923. The station then passed to the London Midland Region of British Railways under the 1948 nationalisation. It was one of only two stations on the Settle & Carlisle line to remain open (Settle being the other) following the withdrawal of local stopping trains in May 1970.

Signal Box : Appleby North signal box opened in 1951 to replace the original signal box on the opposite side of the line, which opened in 1890 but was destroyed by fire. The new box is at the junction for the line to Warcop, which is a remnant of the NER route, having seen regular use until 1989, with freight serving the Army depot at Warcop.

Warcop Branch : The line from Appleby North Junction to Warcop ran for just over six miles via Appleby West Junction. Following the cessation of quarry traffic from Merrygill in the mid 1970s, the remaining section of line was used only by the Army for equipment and troop trains. Other trains did appear on the branch, such as weed-killing trains and railtours.

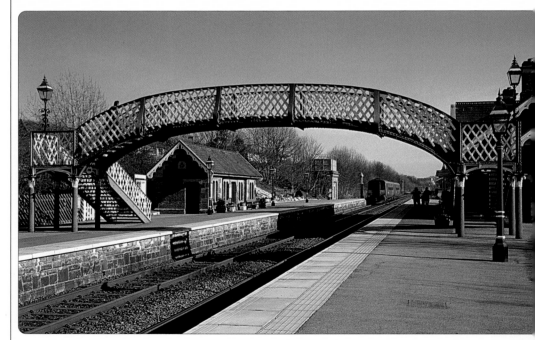

Appleby Station : Looking south on 24th March 2003, Class 156 2-Car 'Super Sprinter' No.15646 (above) heads away from the station after stopping with 2H93, the 14:49 Carlisle - Leeds. **Martin Buck**

Appleby North

The north end of the station, from platform level or on the footbridge, affords good views of southbound trains. This is the view from the 'Down' platform and, on 14th April 2007, Class 60 No.60045 'The Permanent Way Institution' (above) accelerates towards the station with gypsum dust blowing off the train in the process. The train is 6E13, the 12:40 Newbiggin - Milford Sidings.

Note the repositioning of a new semaphore signal gantry directly beside the signal box and that the 'box also has been smartened up with a fresh coat of paint. **Dave McAlone**

On 24th March 2003, looking from the footbridge, Class 158 unit No.158908 (below) enters Appleby station with 1E23, the 14:10 Glasgow Central - Leeds passenger service. **Martin Buck**

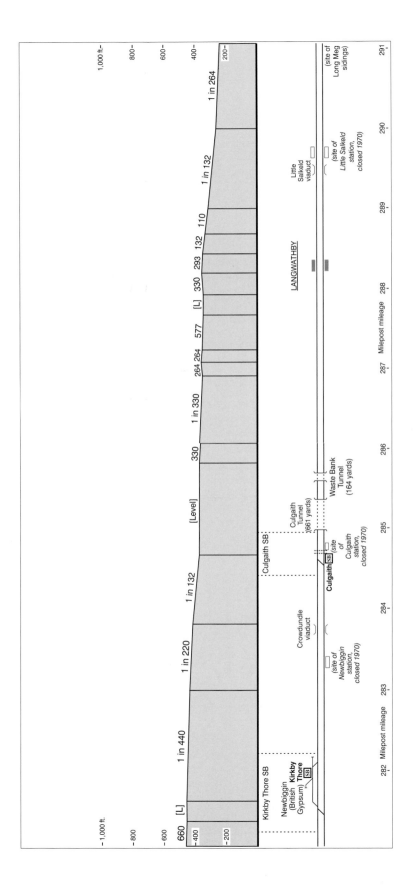

Newbiggin - Long Meg

Newbiggin: It's great to see 'heritage' traction on 'S & C' freight. Although a '56' on the Saturday timber train has become a semi-regular occurrence on the WCML, the diagram hasn't been frequently routed over Ais Gill, so this image is somewhat a rarity! On Saturday, 24th April 2013, No.56105 (above) passes Newbiggin with 6J37, the 12:42 Carlisle Yard - Chirk loaded timber. **John Longden**

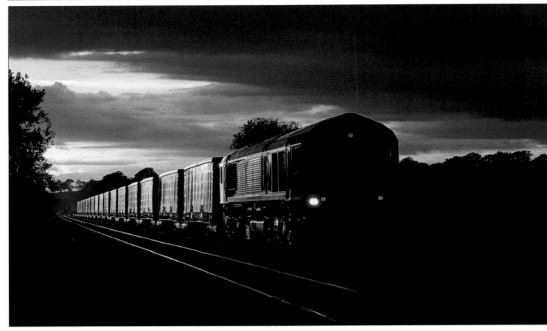

Kirkby Thore

In 2007, a brand new freight flow starts running overnight on the northern end of the line, taking plasterboard from the British Gypsum plant at Kirkby Thore (Newbiggin) to Elderslie, near Glasgow, operated by DRS.

Unfortunately, this service did not run at a good time for the railway photographer. However, around 21:30hrs on the evening of 4th July 2008, there is just about enough light to catch a 'glint' shot of No.66415 (above) slowing down in readiness to reverse into the sidings at Kirkby Thore with 4M78, the 16:07 Elderslie - Newbiggin, formed of a rake of 'British Gypsum' branded curtainsiders. **John Longden**

On 14th April 2007, Virgin Class 57/3 'Thunderbird' No.57308 'Tin Tin' (below) passes the entrance to the British Gypsum plant at the head of 1M81, the diverted 09:18 Glasgow Central - London Euston, towing Pendolino No.390052. **Dave McAlone**

Newbiggin

Other than late autumn, Newbiggin is most photogenic in April, when the warm spring sunshine highlights the scene best and the leaves are still to emerge. On 14th April 2010, a purposeful looking Class 66/0 No.66199 (above) powers through Crowdundle Beck cutting and across the lesser seen viaduct with 6K05, the 12:18 Carlisle Yard - Crewe Basford Hall engineer's working. **John Longden**

Culgaith

An unidentified Virgin Class 47/8 (below) passes Culgaith with a northbound diversion off the WCML on 8th November 1995. The train has passed the signal box and old station buildings and is approaching Culgaith signal box No.3 signal ('Down Starting'), which is carried on a tubular post. **Neil Harvey**

Culgaith

Culgaith railway station was built by the Midland Railway. It opened in 1880 and closed, like so many other stations on the route, in May 1970 when local stopping trains were withdrawn.

The station building sits on a surviving portion of the southbound platform, converted into a private dwelling; most of the remaining station buildings (including the northbound platform) were demolished after closure. These buildings have a completely different appearance from all other stations due to this station being built four years after the others. It was designed by John Holloway Sanders and the style is known as 'Derby Gothic'.

The Station Master had a small cottage, rather than the normal substantial house, and The Midland Railway hadn't intended to build a station serving Culgaith at all, until the local vicar objected.

Signal Box : The signalbox is a Midland Railway type 4a design, built in 1908 to replace an earlier 'box, and controls the first level crossing on the line heading northwards, the only other level crossing being at Low House, just north of Armathwaite

It has a 17 lever Midland Railway Tumbler (Works Relock) frame, which replaced an earlier box, and works Absolute Block to Low House Crossing signal box and Kirkby Thore signal box.

Culgaith Tunnel : Shortly after leaving the site of the old station, about a quarter-of-a-mile, the line enters the south portal of the 661 yards long Culgaith Tunnel, sometimes referred to as Waste Bank No.1 tunnel, built between 1870 - 1873.

(Above) : **Culgaith Signal Box** : Close up view taken in September 1995.

This 'box, along with the one at Settle Junction, has a name board of Midland Railway origin, perhaps dating from the signal box's construction. The mechanism is a 16 lever works-relocked Midland tumbler frame and the first lever (first one visible on the right) is the 'No.1 Down Main Distant', a colour light signal out by Crowdundle viaduct and Park Wood. **Martin Loader**

Culgaith Station, opened in 1880, is pictured as a private residence on 1st November 2011 and, as can be seen, it doesn't conform to the standard Midland template of other 'S & C' stations. A Class 158 + Class 153 combination, with No.158855 (above) leading, heads the 11:55 Carlisle - Leeds passenger service past the disused, but still extant, 'Up' platform.

Class 158 No.158796 (below) heads towards the southern portal of Culgaith Tunnel with the 10:49hrs Leeds - Carlisle, as Class 66/0 No.66167 is about to enter the north portal heading south on a short freight, possibly 6K05 from Carlisle. The date is 5th April 2012. **Dave McAlone (2)**

Staingills

Staingills lies between Culgaith and Langwathby. On 23rd March 2007, Class 60 No.60013 'Robert Boyle' (above) sweeps round the curve under the bridge and into view with 6E13, Newbiggin - Drax gypsum empties, unusually seen heading north and diverted via Carlisle and the Tyne Valley. This was due to the closure of the line for engineering work south of Kirkby Thore.

Langwathby

Class 66/0 No.66138 (below) struggles through blizzard conditions south of Langwathby on 1st December 2010 with 6K05, the 12:18 Carlisle Yard - Crewe Basford Hall departmental, which includes a 'YXA-B' coded 'Windhoff' MPV (Multi Purpose Vehicle) in the consist, immediately behind the loco. **Dave McAlone (2)**

Long Meg

Long Meg Signal Box was located beside the 'Down' main line, south of Eden Lacy viaduct and north of Little Salkeld. It was a London Midland Region Type 15 design fitted with a 40 lever London Midland Region Standard frame, opening on 3rd July 1955. This 'box replaced the Long Meg Sidings Ground Frame, which only connected with the 'Up' line, although there had been a Midland Railway signal box at the location until 13th March 1915.

The signal box, illustrated below, closed on 11th July 1990 when the 'Absolute Block Section' was extended between Culgaith and Low House Crossing signal boxes, but remained in a derelict condition for well over a decade before being demolished.

Long Meg Sidings : These were used by anhydrite trains.

Mining at Long Meg Drift mine started in 1885 by the Long Meg Plaster Company Limited and was connected to the Midland Railway in the following year. Carlisle Plaster and Cement Company Limited closed the mine in 1914/15, which probably explains the closure of the original signal box. In 1922, the mine was reopened for the extraction of anhydrite by the Long Meg Plaster and Mineral Company Limited. The mine was purchased in 1939 and worked by the British Plaster Board Limited (becoming British Gypsum) until closure in January 1976.

Anhydrite mineral trains were once a common sight on the Settle & Carlisle in steam days with BR Class 9f 2-10-0s / Class 8f 2-8-0s working from Long Meg to chemical plants in Widnes, and to Whitehaven. The anhydrite was carried in 2-axle vacuum brake 'UYV' hoppers, purpose built by BREL, Shildon, in the 1950s.

Anhydrite is a mineral - anhydrous calcium sulphate, $CaSO_4$. The name anhydrite was given by A. G. Werner in 1804 because of the absence of water. It is used along with gypsum to produce plaster, wallboard and other products for the construction industry. Anhydrite can also be used as a source of sulphur in the production of sulphuric acid.

Long Meg Sidings Signal Box : For many years, this 'box was 'switched out' before finally closing on 17th November 1983. Over 20 years later, on 4th March 2003, the derelict 'box is passed by the 09:49hrs Leeds – Carlisle, comprising Class 156 No.156454 in an early Northern livery and Class 153 No.153378 (above) nearest the camera and still in Arriva colours with 'Northern' markings. **Dave McAlone**

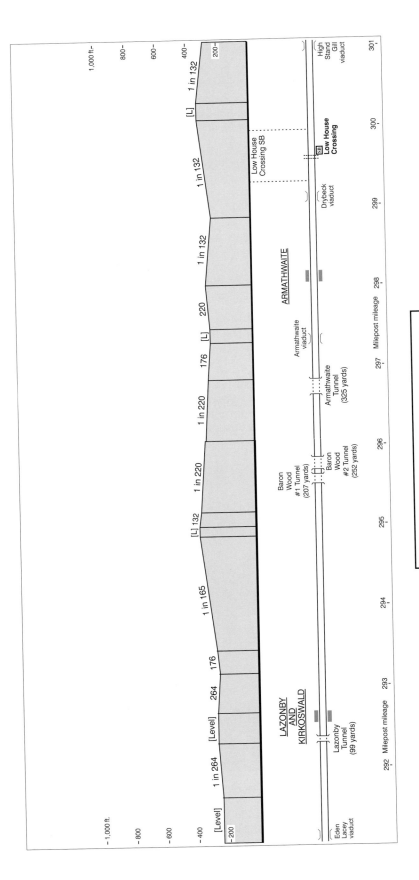

Long Meg - Cotehill

Armathwaite : Due to the closure of the 'S & C' in the south, GBRf Class 66/7 No.66715 'Valour' (above) is seen heading away from the station at Armathwaite on 18th July 2006 with the diverted 4M52, the 06:15 West Burton - Newbiggin loaded gypsum . **Dave McAlone**

Eden Lacy

Twenty minutes behind a FHH empty coal train, this work-a-day DBS diagram toils north through the Eden Valley. On 5th August 2011, Class 66/0 No.66034 (above) is seen on the attractive stretch of line between Eden Lacy and Lazonby with 4S93, the 15:04 Milford - New Cumnock 'HTA' coal empties. This small stretch of the 'S & C' is on an embankment, clear of trees, and abounds with photographic possibilities

Not that you would know, but the clouds you can see advancing from the north held the heaviest snowfall seen for over a decade and, that night (26th November 2010), the 'S & C' was transformed into a winter wonderland with the snow staying for a long time! Beforehand, however, before heading home to 'batten down the hatches' there was time to catch Colas Class 66/8 No.66842 (below) heading south near Eden Lacy House with 6J37, the 12:50 Carlisle Yard - Chirk log train.

John Longden (2)

Lazonby Tunnel

(North Portal) : This is the view (above) of the entrance to the 99-yards long Lazonby Tunnel, in front of which is Intermediate Block Signal No.LH10, controlled by Low House Crossing signal box.

(South Portal) : Emerging from the southern portal on 14th July 2011 is FHH Class 66/6 No.66605 (below) heading for the East Midlands; 6M11, the 04:38 Killoch - Ratcliffe coal train.   **Dave McAlone (2)**

Lazonby & Kirkoswald

The station's Northern Rail station sign (opposite), set amongst a splendid floral display, frames the Celtic cross atop the graveyard of St Nicholas' Church, which is a parish church forming a united benefice with churches at nearby Great Salkeld and Kirkoswald. 13th July 2011.

On the following day, Class 66/8 No.66843 (above) passes through Lazonby with the 6J37 'logs' where, in the right hand background, St. Nicholas' church tower can be seen along with the Celtic Cross, looking down on the graveyard.
Dave McAlone (2)

Armathwaite

...nathwaite signal box, opened in July 1899, closed in 1983 and was restored in 1992 to its original Midland ...way design by the Friends of the Settle-Carlisle Railway, albeit it is now non-operational. The yellow and ... colours are authentic. On 14th June 2012, FHH Class 66/5 No.66598 (above) passes the 'box heading ...21, the 10:03 Killoch - West Burton coal train.

...pposite) : In the beautiful Eden Valley, Class 66/0 No.66246 powers an unidentified train of loaded coal ...pers on 6th July 2006, negotiating the reverse curves to the south of Armathwaite station.

Drybeck Viaduct

...s viaduct was built between 1871 - 1874, stands 80 feet high above the ground and is 139 yards long with ...en arches. On 26th May 2007, Class 57/3 No.57311 'Parker' (below) heads the diverted 1M81, 09:18 ...sgow Central - London Euston across the viaduct, with Pendolino No.390006 in tow. **Dave McAlone (3)**

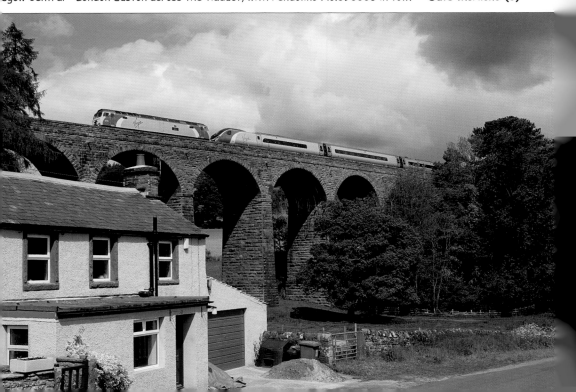

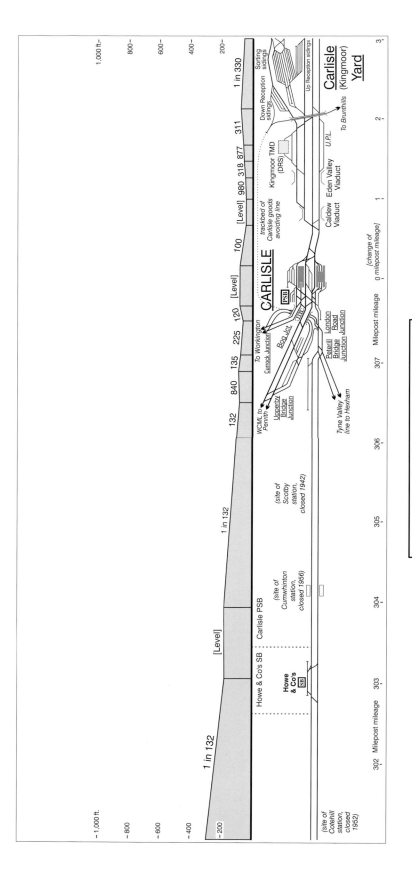

Cotehill - Carlisle

Carlisle Citadel : Looking smart under the impressive gantry of signals at the south end of Carlisle Citadel station, Colas Class 66/8 No.66843 (above) waits to depart with 6J37, the 12:50 Carlisle Yard – Chirk timber on 28th February 2011. **Kenny Marrs**

Cotehill

We're on the last stretch of the 'S & C', about five miles before the line joins the Tyne Valley line from Newcastle at Petteril Bridge Junction. At Duncowfold, near Cotehill, the old telegraph poles are still extant well into the 21st Century, as Class 66/0 No.66101 (above) passes on 31st May 2011 with 6K05, the 12:18 Carlisle Yard - Crewe Basford Hall departmental service.

Cumwhinton

This station closed in 1956, although both platforms and former waiting shelter survive - it was Grade II listed in 1984! On 2nd April 2009, Class 66/0 No.66067 (below) heads 6K05 and a long rake of Low Sided Open Box Wagons, of the type coded 'MCA', 'MDA', 'MLA' and 'MOA'. **Dave McAlone (2)**

CARLISLE

Durran Hill : Minutes behind the Clitheroe cement service (6M00), Class 66/0 No.66086 (above) appears with 6E85, Hunterston - Drax loaded coal on 3rd April 2009, throwing a long plume of exhaust into the clear spring air, as the GM machine prepares for the 'Long Drag'. There used to be extensive sidings at Durran Hill, plus a Midland Railway steam roundhouse, which was a subshed of Carlisle Kingmoor.   **John Longden**

London Road : 4M52, the 06:15 West Burton - Newbiggin gypsum has been diverted over the Tyne Valley route due to the closure of the 'S & C' for engineering work. It is seen backing in to London Road Yard on 23rd March 2007, where GBRf Class 66/7 No.66723 (below) will run round and back out of the yard to face Petteril Bridge Junction, the divergence of which can just be made out to the left of the loco. **Dave McAlone**

Bog Junction - London Road Junction

At the time of this picture, 11th April 2011, there was no regular use of the route from the Cumbrian Coast to Upperby. However, between 28th March 2011 - 17th July 2011, due to essential maintenance work on Kent Viaduct, Arnside, Sellafield flask services were diverted via Workington, Upperby and Shap.

Here, DRS Class 37s No.37682 + 37229 'Jonty Jarvis' (above) pass under the WCML with 6K73, the 14:40 Sellafield - Crewe flasks, alongside the little used goods lines on the right which still carry occasional flask trains to Seaton on Tees. These lines have diverged from Bog Junction and will join the North East passenger line (curving up to Carlisle station on the right) at London Road Junction.

The rusted looking lines lead to Bog Junction, which can just be made out underneath the WCML overbridge, on which a DMU is seen leaving for the Cumbrian Coast. On 26th May 2007, Class 57/3 No.57314 (below) trundles down from Carlisle South Junction to London Road Junction with 1M87, 13:10 Glasgow Central - London Euston, formed by Pendolino No.390014, diverted via the Settle & Carlisle route. **Dave McAlone (2)**

(Right) : The *Carlisle Citadel Act* of 1861 provided for a new loop between Bog Junction and Willowholme Junction to take goods traffic away from the station. This line came into use in 1877, a joint venture by the Caledonian, Glasgow & South Western, Midland Railway and the London North Western Railway Companies.

Class 25 No.25185 (right) is crossing the River Caldew on the old Joint Goods lines with a short freight heading for the 'S & C'. The bridge survived after the goods line closed and became part of a cycle route.

CARLISLE 'AVOIDING' LINE

Until May 1984, an 'avoiding' line took freight traffic away from busy Citadel station, running from Caldew Junction (3/4-mile north of Citadel station on the WCML) to Rome Street; a junction leading to Currock junction (Cumbrian Coast traffic), London Road Junction (Tyne Valley / the 'S & C') and Upperby Junction (for WCML). Unfortunately, a serious accident (not fatal) sealed its fate ....

On the morning of 1st May 1984, a section of a Liverpool - Glasgow freightliner broke away in the Petteril Valley and, having initially been left behind, the breakaway vehicles gained speed on the 1 in 184 / 131 gradient and, when the driver braked for a crew change in Citadel station, he was unaware of what had happened.

A major pile up was avoided by a quick-thinking signalman in Carlisle PSB, who switched the runaway portion onto the 'avoiding line'. The vehicles were probably doing 60 - 70mph when they passed Rome Street junction and then derailed at the next curve, falling into the River Caldew (see below), demolishing part of the bridge in the process. The bridge and line were never resurrected and now all freight traffic has to pass through the bottleneck, which is Carlisle Citadel station.

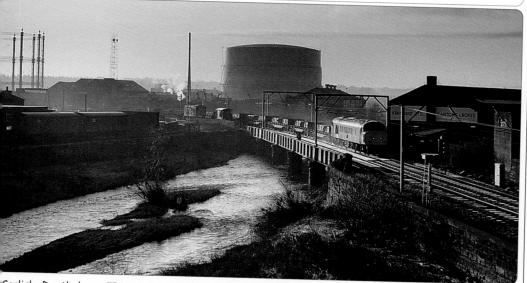

Carlisle Dentholme : This is a view, taken on 2nd February 1983, looking from Nelson bridge towards Rome Street Junction. On the left, some vans are in the Metal Box sidings and a Class 08 loco passes with a short 'trip' working. Meanwhile, Class 46, No.46017 (above) crosses Caldew Viaduct with a heavy steel train from the North East. This is the point of the derailment in May 1984.   **Dave McAlone (2)**

CARLISLE CITADEL

Arrivals & Departures

Carlisle Citadel is a 'gateway' to Scotland, the North East, Cumbrian Coast, WCML south and the Settle & Carlisle to Leeds. The station platforms reflect these services:

Platform 1 : Relief West Coast Main Line platform (bi-directional).

Platform 2 : Cumbrian Coast Line bay platform.

Platform 3 : West Coast Main Line north-bound platform (bi-directional).

Platform 4 : West Coast Main Line south-bound platform (bi-directional).

Platform 5 : Tyne Valley Line bay.

Platform 6 : Carlisle to Leeds Line bay.

Platforms 7 & 8 : Local Scottish services between Carlisle and Glasgow bays.

The magnificent canopy is a feature of Citadel station, which allows plenty of light to shine through. On 10th September 2013, DRS Malcolm-liveried Class 66/4 No.66434 (above) proceeds along Platform 4 road with 6K05, the 12:18 Carlisle Yard - Crewe Basford Hall departmental service.   **Kenny Marrs**

(Opposite) : Class 66/0 No.66059 (top left) arrives at Carlisle Citadel station having come over the 'Long Drag' with 6S89, the 13:55 Milford Sidings - Ayr MGR empties. The train will go forward to Carlisle Yard where it will be 'staged' along with other MGR services using the ex-Glasgow & South Western route (via Dumfries) for crew change and pathing purposes. July 2003.   **Martin Buck**

Meanwhile, on 15th May 2012, FHH Class 66/5 No.66547 (bottom left) snakes into Carlisle with 4S33, Drax - Carstairs Down Sidings 'HXA' coal empties; the 'HXAs' were built in 2006 by Wagony Swidnica, Poland, a shorter version of the 'HHA' coal hopper, but carry the same payload.   **Kenny Marrs**

Also standing at Platform 4, on 5th April 1988, two Class 31/4s fitted with Electric Train Supply, No.31410 + No.31429 (below), wait to leave Carlisle with the 16:10hrs service to Leeds.   **Neil Harvey**

Carlisle Citadel Railwayana

Carlisle Citadel station was built in 1847, in a neo-Tudor style, designed by William Tite. To commemorate the station's 150th Anniversary in 1997, six murals (above) were commissioned for the east wall alongside two bay platforms, which are used by local services to Leeds and the Tyne Valley.   **Martin Buck**

Southbound departures from Platforms 3 and 4, plus the two 'Up & Down' Sidings, are controlled by a gantry of four Multiple Aspect Colour Light Signals (below) which straddle the four lines.   **Keith McGovern**

The
Lure
of
Steam

'S & C' Steam Timeline

1968 : **'Fifteen Guinea Special' (1T57)**. The last main-line passenger train to be hauled by a steam loco on British Railways runs on 11 August 1968, prior to the introduction of a steam ban the following day. The special train runs from Liverpool to Carlisle and back, via the Settle & Carlisle, featuring BR Standard Pacific 4-6-2 No.70013 'Oliver Cromwell' on the outward journey and LMS 'Black Five' 4-6-0s No.44781 + No.44871 double-heading on the return.

1972 : Steam ban lifted, although the 'S & C' still prohibited due, primarily, to steam locos not being allowed into Carlisle Citadel station 'under the wires' following electrification in 1974.

1978 : A momentous year - steam is allowed to run into Carlisle, albeit subject to very tight guidelines and on 25th March 1978, LNER V2 2-6-2 No.4771 'Green Arrow' becomes the first steam loco to return to the 'S & C'.

1979 : Penmanshiel Tunnel disaster sees an increase in East Coast traffic diverted over the 'S & C', which results in no steam specials throughout 1979.

1980 : Steam returns to the 'S & C' with the 'Cumbrian Mountain Express'

This regular steam working on a Saturday was operated then by SLOA (Steam Locomotive Operators Association) from London Euston to Carlisle using 'Steamtown'-based steam engines; one working Carnforth - Carlisle and the other Carlisle - Hellifield.

1994 : British Rail is privatised and with it go a lot of the restrictions regarding mainline steam running. The West Coast Railways Company (WCRC) is established and, by opting for Carnforth as its base, is well placed for 'S & C' steam operations. In fact, in 1998, WCRC became the first privately owned company to be given a licence as a Train Operating Company.

There are now regular steam-hauled excursions over the 'S & C'.

LMS Midland Railway 1000 Class 4-4-0

Midland Compound No.1000 (above) arrives at Hellifield on the 4th February 1983 on the first of two weekends featuring this loco and 'Leander' on the 'S & C'. The northbound run leaves Hellifield extremely late due to the late arrival of the road tanker supplying water for the loco.   **Neil Harvey**

LMS Stanier Class 8f 2-8-0

(Previous page) : To begin this feature, Class 8f No.48151 leaves Settle Junction behind and starts the arduous 15-mile climb (1 in 100) to Blea Moor on 11th July 2012 with 'The Fellsman'.   **Neil Harvey**

LNER Thompson Class B1 4-6-0

No.1264 and Class 8F 2-8-0 No.48151 (above) wait to leave Hellifield on the 8th June 1999 marking the ɑsion of the first test run of No.1264, having been restored to main line condition after many year's work. 48151 was included for 'insurance', but in the end everything went OK and it wasn't needed.

LNER K4 Class 2-6-0 'Mogul'

61994 'The Great Marquess' (below) struggles past Greengates, near Birkett alongside Mallerstang Edge, ɦ the return 'Fellsman' charter (1Z53, 15:34 Carlisle to Lancaster) on 19th June, suffering from a build-ɨof ash in the smokebox. It later stops at Garsdale for the front end to be cleaned out, as the char was ɘcting the smokebox vacuum.   **Neil Harvey (2)**

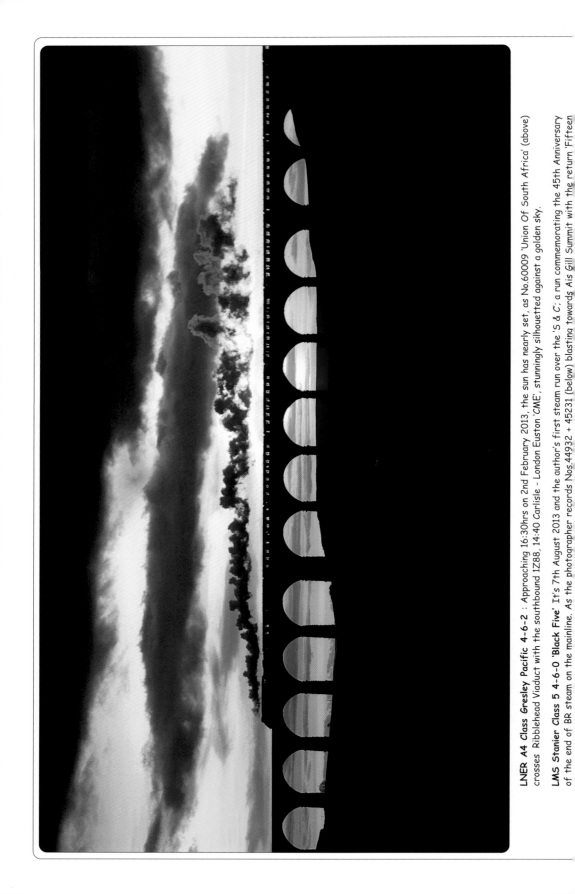

LNER A4 Class Gresley Pacific 4-6-2 : Approaching 16:30hrs on 2nd February 2013, the sun has nearly set, as No.60009 'Union Of South Africa' (above) crosses Ribblehead Viaduct with the southbound 1Z88, 14:40 Carlisle - London Euston 'CME', stunningly silhouetted against a golden sky.

LMS Stanier Class 5 4-6-0 'Black Five' It's 7th August 2013 and the author's first steam run over the 'S & C'; a run commemorating the 45th Anniversary of the end of BR steam on the mainline. As the photographer records Nos.44932 + 45231 (below) blasting towards Ais Gill Summit with the return 'Fifteen

LMS 'Jubilee' Class 4-6-0

MS maroon No.5690 'Leander'
ght) roars through Settle Jct.
17th August 2008. The train is
10, 11:32 Hellifield - Carlisle.

eam-hauled expresses could
ill be seen on the 'S & C' upto a
ar before the end of BR steam.
owever, in 1967, steam was
stricted to two northbound
mmer Saturday relief trains,
agrammed for Holbeck based
ubilees'. Luckily, four survive:

.45593 'Kolhapur'
.45596 'Bahamas'
.45690 'Leander'
.45699 'Galatea'

Neil Harvey

GWR 'Castle' Class 4-6-0

e first GWR steam loco to make an appearance on the 'S & C' was on 12th February 1994, in the shape of
.5029 'Nunney Castle' (top left), which is seen making a spectacular crossing of Ribblehead Viaduct.
e northbound run proves to be extremely laboured and, on the return journey, she comes to a standstill
Kirby Stephen due to wheel slip, resulting in diesel assistance and a two-hour delay!   **Michael McNicholas**

LMS 'Royal Scot' Class 4-6-0

.46115 'Scots Guardsman' was purchased by the WCRC in 2008, restored to main-line running standard in
Brunswick Green livery, and hauled her first railtour on 16th August 2008 from Hellifield to Carlisle and
ck. On 7th February 2009, No.46115 (above) is seen at Blea Moor with the outward 'Cumbrian Fellsman'
om Manchester Victoria to Carlisle.   **Neil Harvey**

o days later, this time between Blea Moor signal box and Blea Moor tunnel. Having travelled over 350 miles
a round trip to see 'Scots Guardsman' (bottom left) travelling north over the 'S & C', conditions couldn't
better, sun, snow and steam. In getting here, the snow in places was above the knees!   **Keith McGovern**

LMS 'Princess Royal' Class 4-6-2 Pacific

This Class of express passenger steam loco by William Stanier are Pacifics (i.e. 4-6-2 wheel arrangement) and 13 examples were built at Crewe Works, between 1933 and 1935. Two are preserved and both are illustrated on this page. No.6201 'Princess Elizabeth' (above) is seen at Blea Moor on 12th April 2003 with 1Z62, the 08:52 Bangor - Carlisle 'Cumbrian Mountain Express' (CME), which she works from Chester.

Meanwhile, No.46203 'Princess Margaret Rose' (below) coasts south through Langcliffe, near Settle, with a return 'CME' on 22nd June 1991. This loco was No.6203 prior to BR nationalisation in 1948, thereafter No.46203 until withdrawal in 1962. It was bought by Billy Butlin of Butlin's holiday camps.

LMS 'Princess Coronation' Class 4-6-2 Pacific

The locos in this Class are also known as 'Duchesses'. No.6233 'Duchess of Sutherland' was outshopped in July 1938 from Crewe Works in LMS standard crimson lake livery, fitted with a single chimney and without smoke deflectors. Here, No.6233 (above), with smoke deflectors, passes Settle Junction with 1Z62, the 13:15 Carlisle - Preston on the 9th July 2005. Next stop Long Preston to take water.

On 3 March 2012, No.6233 was repainted in Brunswick green and, running as No.46233 (below), she passes the site of Crosby Garrett station on 22nd May 2013 with 1Z89, 14:28 Carlisle - Euston 'CME'. She was given her BR number 46233 in October 1948 and was allocated to Crewe North shed.   **Neil Harvey (4)**

LNER A4 Class Gresley Pacific 4-6-2

With Pen-y-Ghent prominent in the background, No.60007 'Sir Nigel Gresley' (above) passes Selside Far Moor in very windy conditions on 1st November 2008; the photographer being on the wrong side of the line to escape a faceful of smoke and clag. Withdrawn from BR service in February 1966, she was saved from the cutter's torch by the A4 Locomotive Society and moved to Crewe for refurbishment. At the time, No.60007 received three pairs of 6ft 8ins driving wheels from sister A4 No.60026 'Miles Beevor', because they were in far better condition.

BR Rebuilt 'West Country' Class Pacific 4-6-2

Atmosphere aplenty as No.34027 'Taw Valley' (below) heads south at Newbiggin on 5th March 1994 with a 'CME'. This was the first Southern Region loco to visit the 'S & C' after 1989, other Southern Pacific locos to make an appearance since then have included No.34027 'Taw Valley' and No.34067 'Tangmere'.

BR Standard Class 4 4-6-0

On 31st March 1995, No.75024 (above) pilots BR Standard Class 7 Pacific No.70000 'Britannia' on the approach to Ais Gill Summit. The train was *'The Final Curtain'* to commemorate the end of the BR Special Trains Unit, running from Carlisle to Liverpool. No.75014 was discovered to have a broken cotter pin shortly after this photograph was taken and 'Britannia' essentially pushed No.75014 all the way to Liverpool!

BR Standard Class 7 4-6-2 Pacific

This locomotive was the last main line engine to receive a repair at Crewe, emerging from the Works in February 1967 .... immortalised forever, when it worked the Manchester Victoria - Carlisle leg of the famous 'Fifteen Guinea Special', the BR main line steam finale on 11th August 1968. Over 40 years later, and still going strong, No.70013 'Oliver Cromwell' (below) blasts out of the north portal of Blea Moor tunnel on 12th September 2009 with a 1Z71, 06:04 Stevenage - Carlisle charter.   **Neil Harvey (4)**

BR Standard Class 8 4-6-2 Pacific

'The Duke' - No.71000 'Duke of Gloucester' (above) puts up a nice bit of clag at the head of a southbound Cumbrian Mountain Express at Birkett Common on the 6th August 1994. Designed by Robert Riddles for use by British Railways, it was constructed in 1954 at Crewe Works. 'The Duke' was a replacement for the destroyed Princess Royal Class loco No.46202 'Princess Anne', which was involved in the Harrow and Wealdstone rail disaster of 1952.

LNER Peppercorn Class A1 4-6-2 Pacific

Well, here she is, the last steam loco to be built - No.60163 'Tornado' - unveiled to the public in 2008 to coincide with the 40th anniversary of the end of BR steam in 1968. On 10th October 2009, No.60163 (below) approaches Ribblehead with 'The Cumbrian Mountain Tornado' from Worcester Shrub Hill to Carlisle. The steam loco took over from DBS Class 66/0 No.66152 at Hellifield. **Neil Harvey (2)**

Diesel Excursions over the Fells

Whilst the 'S & C', with its stunning scenery and arduous climbs, lends itself to the magic of steam, the line also sees its fair share of diesel-hauled excursions, attracting locos not normally associated with it. Perhaps, not so spectacular as steam, but interesting and diverse all the same. These tours range from the basic enthusiast charter to the luxury 'wine & dine' market, such as the 'Orient Express, 'Northern Belle' and 'Royal Scotsman'.

As far as rolling stock is concerned, at the time of the line's reprieve in 1989, the 'BR Blue' era was in full swing and you would have been hard pressed to see anything other than the ubiquitous corporate blue & grey coaching stock. Since then, especially following the privatisation of British Rail in 1994, privately owned coaches have become commonplace to brighten things up. There's traditional Mk1 stock painted in 1960s maroon livery, 1950s carmine and cream, chocolate & cream, plus Southern Region green to be seen, too.

This portfolio gives a flavour of the variety of loco classes to visit the Settle & Carlisle.

Class 46 : No.D172 'Ixion' (left) exits Birkett Tunnel on 20th July 1996 with a 'Cumbrian Mountain Express' returning to Salisbury. It is substituting for LMS 4-6-2 No.46229 'Duchess of Hamilton' due to the risk of lineside fires!

Class 52 : The noise from the two Maybach engines was awesome, just a shame about the dismal weather! On 31st July 2010, the maroon liveried No.D1015 'Western Champion' (below) passes Stockber with 1Z53, the 14:45 Appleby - Westbury.　　　　**Neil Harvey (2)**

Class 20 : The sun refuses to play ball on 7th February 2009 as DRS Class 20s No.20303 + No.20304 (above) head north across Selside Far Moor with a Spitfire Railtours charter; the 1Z20, 07:22 Birmingham International - Carlisle 'Fellsman Chopper'. A WCRC Class 47 is on the rear of the train to provide some much needed warmth for the passengers onboard!

Neil Harvey

Class 40 : This was a personal invite that I was only too pleased to accept, a ride behind No.D200 (40122) on its first outing following its reprieve. It is pictured at Dent (below) on 31st July 1983 during a photo-stop with 1Z12, the 08:48 London King's Cross - Carlisle 'Hadrian Pullman'. Withdrawn in August 1981, the pioneer 'whistler' was restored at Toton TMD using the power unit from No.40076.

Martin Buck

Class 37 : These venerable machines are always a popular choice with enthusiasts and on 20th June 2009, Class 37/4 No.37401 + Class 37/6 No.37670 'St. Blazey T & RS Depot' (above) storm past Settle Junction with 1Z21, the 15:04 York - Carlisle, which is the second leg of 'The Jorvik Fellsman'. A uniform rake of Mk2f vehicles in Virgin red livery adds to the spectacle.

Class 43 'HST' : There cannot have been too many times a Great Western HST set has ventured onto 'S & C' metals but, on 31st May 1997, one does .... Class 43 power car No.43179 (below), in the original post-privatisation First Great Western livery, leads across Lunds Viaduct with a Plymouth - Carlisle charter. This view clearly shows the 5 arches of the 83 feet high and 103 yards long viaduct.   **Neil Harvey (2)**

Class 37s : No.37698 + No.37668 (above) in Loadhaul black & orange and EWS red livery, respectively, pass Selside beneath a snow-covered Pen-y-Ghent with 1Z71, the 06:10 Crewe - Carlisle 'Festive Excursion' on 29th December 2003; the 37s well into the 1 in 100 'Long Drag' to Ais Gill summit.   **Neil Harvey**

Class 40 : Preserved Class 40 No.40145 (below) looks resplendent in Brunswick green livery crossing Lunds Viaduct on 12th July 2003 with 1Z41, the 14:49 Carlisle - Birmingham International 'Pennine Fellsman'. Note the footbridge on the left which, in addition to allowing a footpath to cross the line, is also the sole access to a house, just out of view to the left. This explains the blue car in the field!   **Martin Loader**

Class 55 : Just stunning .... when everything comes together there's no other way to describe it. A great railtour with classic traction, matching stock and favourable timings for the photographer, for once in good weather. In BR Blue livery, No.55022 'Royal Scots Grey' (above) thunders through Garsdale on 31st May 2010 with the 'Deltic Retro Scot II' railtour (running as 1Z87, Stockport - Edinburgh and return); outward via the 'S & C' and return via the ECML.   **John Longden**

Class 56 : Hideous or a welcome new livery? Colourful Hanson Traction Class 56 No.56312 'Artemis' (below), plus No.66148, roar through Garsdale station with 1Z66, the 05:41 Bristol Temple Meads 'Scenic Settler' railtour on 22nd May 2010. The Class 56 came on the train at Birmingham New Street.   **Neil Harvey**

Class 47 : Class 47/7 No.47739 'Resourceful' (above) brings a splash of red to an otherwise green and blue vista, as it passes Foredale, near Helwith Bridge, on 22nd January 2000, with a charter from London King's Cross to Carlisle and York. Today, No.47739 is now part of the ColasRail fleet of locos, which includes another two Class 47s, No.47727 and No.47749.

Class 50 : Nos.50024 'Vanguard' + No.50050 'Fearless' (below) pass Smardale with the return leg of the 'Fellsman II' railtour, 1Z41, the 12:20 Carlisle - Taunton on 23rd April 1988. Unfortunately, No.50024 failed early into the tour and did not power on the outward climb over Shap and the return over Ais Gill. 'Fellsman 1' ran (successfully!) on 30th January 1988 with Nos.50008 'Thunderer' + 50034 'Furious'.   **Neil Harvey (2)**

Personal
Recollections

Setting the Scene

The Settle & Carlisle has always been one of my favourite railway lines but, living over 200 miles away, I was never able to make as many visits as I would have liked. My association with the 'S & C' started with a five day photographic trip way back in the summer of 1979, followed by two subsequent trips, one later that year and one final sojourn in 1980. I set out to photograph 'S & C' freight but, as many other visitors have found, I was thwarted by one thing for which the 'S & C' is renowned for - very changeable weather! However, I was able to bring back a few treasured memories and I would like to share a small selection of scanned 35mm photographs with you.

After this, save for a brief visit to the line in 2003, I turned my attention to travelling over the line. I wanted to see the splendid scenery through the carriage window, preferably hauled by an English Electric Class 40 loco. There were, sadly, too few opportunities, but I have included a few noteworthy experiences.

June 1979

This is when my love affair with the 'S & C' first started, driving from Swindon to Garsdale, for a week-long visit and to try out camping for the first time.

Unfortunately, the camping part was the first setback .....

.... trying to pitch a tent after a visit to the Moorcock Inn for some evening refreshment was not a good idea, resulting in alternative accommodation for the night being sought!

Photographically speaking, I was naive and ill-equipped - just a basic, Chinon 35mm Instamatic camera, which lacked both shutter speed and aperture controls - it was simply aim, shoot and hope for the best! A lot of blurred photographs, but a handful worth keeping all the same.

I had no knowledge of the best photographic locations or how to get to them, so photographs were restricted to station shots or where line passed close to a road; Ais Gill readily springs to mind.

First Impressions Count

Blea Moor : Having left the car underneath the arches of Ribblehead viaduct, it was a brisk walk to Blea Moor signal box and, as luck would have it, the signalman on duty kindly allowed me to come inside and see the operation of a 30 lever frame in operation - a wonderful experience. Having watched Class 40 No.40070 pull up alongside the 'box with 6E53, the 10:31 Ribblehead Quarry - Healey Mills ballast, I thanked the signalman and quickly positioned myself for a shot of No.40070 (above) leaving Blea Moor, bang on time at 11:07hrs, with a rake of loaded 2-axle 'ZEV'/'ZFV' (Dogfish) and 'YGH' (Sealion) wagons.

Although the 'S & C' closed to regular through freight traffic in May 1983, ballast trains from Ribblehead continued to traverse the southern section for a further 18-months.

(Previous Page) :

The Viaduct : This was my first view of the 'S & C', driving along the B6255 road from Ingleton, and what a sight it was too ..... the incredible 24-arch Ribblehead Viaduct (bottom) standing 165ft high above the valley of the River Ribble. A lone 'Down Main' Distant signal stood tall at the north end of the viaduct guarding the approach to Blea Moor, almost indiscernible below the mass of Whernside.

The Signal (top right) controls passage at Blea Moor for northbound trains. It is a 'Two Way' Bracket signal where the primary signal (Upper Quadrant) is for the 'Down Main' line and the lower 'miniature arm' gives access to the 'Down' Passing Loop. Both signal gantry and passing loop have long since gone.

Ais Gill : An early start and low cloud lingers over Wild Boar Fell on 7th June 1979 as Carlisle Kingmoor Class 40, No.40098 (top left), strolls into view, about to pass under the B6259 road bridge, with 8G80, the 06:00 Carlisle Yard - Bescot. Hopefully, a foretaste of things to come!

Appleby

Having set back into the sidings by Appleby signal box to allow 7E84, the 07:30 Carlisle - Tinsley to pass, Class 25 No.25322 (above) now shunts the daily 9T20, 08:10 Carlisle - Warcop 'trip'.

Kirkby Stephen

It's a long way from home and I did not expect to see a Cardiff Canton based Class 47, No.47078 'Sir Daniel Gooch' (below), turning up on the first northbound express of the day - 1S49, the 07:15 Nottingham - Glasgow Central - which is seen passing Kirkby Stephen on 3rd September 1979.

September 1979

1979 proved to be a momentous year; Trevor Francis signs for Nottingham Forest in British football's first £1 million deal, Margaret Thatcher became Britain's first woman Prime Minister and, overseas, the Shah of Iran is overthrown leading to an Islamic republic under the Grand Ayatollah Khomeini.

As far me, a second visit to the 'S & C' in 1979 (w/c Monday, 3rd September) was less momentous and a bitter-sweet affair as, unbeknown to me, the line was to close completely on the Thursday and Friday, so that the railway bridge across the A66 road at Appleby could be replaced.

Anglo-Scottish expresses ran for the first three days, along with a modicum of freight traffic, but most had already been cancelled or diverted off route. Needless to say, this was extremely disappointing, especially as the weather was good initially with long spells of sunshine and a favourable forecast for the rest of the week - c'est la vie!

I had also learnt from my dismal results in June and upgraded my camera equipment; a Fujica SLR (Single Lens Reflex) fitted with a standard 55mm lens, plus a 135mm telephoto lens. Some better results, but I would have to wait until the following year before trying again.

Garsdale

Most freight services were entrusted to the 'big' locos: 40s, 45s, 46s and 47s although the occasional 'small engine' did turn up from time to time, like on Monday, 3rd September 1979, when Class 25 No.25304 (above) entered Garsdale with an unidentified freight working.

Meanwhile, later that same morning, 'split-box' Class 40 No.40139 (overleaf, page 144), enters the station with another unidentified freight. It does, however, include two Italian refrigerated wagons in the consist, which presumably came from the Continent via Dover or Harwich.

Dent

At this time, the semaphore signals at Dent were already 'locked out' as were the ones at Ais Gill; only Garsdale 'box offered 'semi-permanent' control in an otherwise unbroken 17-mile 'block section' between Blea Moor and Kirkby Stephen. This used to be the 'Up' 'Thames-Clyde Express' to London St. Pancras (1M86), but now the 11:50hrs from Glasgow Central only runs to Nottingham. It is seen here running through a closed Dent station on 5th September hauled by Class 47/3 No.47311 (top left), one of Sheffield Tinsley's freight locos.

Meanwhile, looking in the opposite direction, Class 40 No.40199 (bottom left) approaches with 8M64, the 12:35 Healey Mills - Carlisle Yard freight. The magnificent Arten Gill viaduct stands proudly in the distance, which featured in a scene in the movie "Miss Potter" – the Beatrix Potter biopic starring Renee Zellweger, as she travelled from London to the Lake District.

June 1980

Third time, lucky?

Some more annual leave, commencing 2nd June, and a full five days spent photographing in what was, for the most part, good weather. This proved to be a good time to visit the 'S & C' as, by 1982, only two passenger trains a day would remain and there would be only minimal freight. The last scheduled freight traffic ran in 1983 and it would be another 10 years before freight would once again grace the line, and then only a couple of gypsum trains to Newbiggin.

To provide a guide on the level of loco-hauled activity on the Settle & Carlisle in 1980, I have prepared a 24-hour timetable showing passing times at Blea Moor; a reasonable volume, but considerably less than in previous years and levels which would not be seen again!

At this time, there were three loco-hauled passenger services in each direction running between Nottingham and Glasgow Central. Two of these, 1M86 and 1S68, were the respective 'Up' and 'Down' reporting codes for the former "Thames Clyde Express" which used to run over the Settle & Carlisle between London St. Pancras and Glasgow Central.

'The Summit'

Was a train coming? You could not tell, as Ais Gill signal box was already unmanned (closing officially in 1981) and the semaphore signals were permanently locked in the 'off' position. However, in the still Cumbrian air, a Class 40-hauled freight train could be heard coming for miles, working flat out on the arduous climb to the summit', such as No.40176 (above) which is seen here breasting the summit on 4th June 1980 with a heavy 7A09, 11:31 Carlisle Yard - Willesden. Note the white painted panel on the bridge behind the signal, known by northbound drivers as the "Star of Bethlehem", positioned there to improve visibility of the signal in front of the bridge

Lunds

This is one of my favourite photographs and a favourite location - *Lunds* - affording clear views of the final stretch of climb to Ais Gill. In this view, No.40175 (previous page) slogs up the embankment across Lunds Viaduct on 4th June 1980 with 7M86, the 20:50 St. Blazey - Carlisle. There are covered china clay wagons from Goonbarrow Junction (Bugle in Cornwall) behind the loco which are destined for the Wiggins Teape paper mill at Corpach in the West Highlands of Scotland. This particular train service boasts the longest journey, both in terms of time and mileage - 20 hours to complete some 480 miles!

BLEA MOOR   June 1980

Time	Code	Train		Notes	
UP					
02:47	1M65,	22:45	Glasgow Central – Nottingham	MX	Parcels
03:32	7M13,	01:35	Carlisle Yard – Toton	MSX	
05:17	6O29,	03:20	Carlisle Yard – Eastleigh	MSX	Merchandise
06:38	6V93,	00:55	Mossend – Severn Tunnel Junction	MX	ABS
08:00 Cement	6M34,	06:30	Carlisle London Road – Earles Sidings	MX	Empty
08:12	8G80,	06:30	Carlisle Yard – Bescot	MSX	
08:42	8G80,	06:30	Carlisle Yard – Bescot	MO	
09:35	7E84,	07:30	Carlisle Yard – Tinsley	SX	(WC)
10:02	7V30,	08:05	Carlisle Yard – Severn Tunnel Junction	SX	
10:39	**1M70,**	**07:05**	**Glasgow Central – Nottingham**		**Passenger**
11:11	6E54,	10:31	Ribblehead – Healey Mills	SX	Ballast (RR)
11:33	7A09,	09:34	Carlisle Yard – Willesden	SX	
14:17	7V00,	12:20	Carlisle Yard – Severn Tunnel Junction	SX	
14:34	**1M86,**	**11:50**	**Glasgow Central – Nottingham**		**Passenger** X)
16:55	8E15,	14:43	Carlisle Yard – Healey Mills	SX	
19:42	**1M87,**	**16:10**	**Glasgow Central – Nottingham**		**Passenger**
20:37	7G02,	18:40	Carlisle Yard – Bescot	SX	
DOWN					
01:00	6M29,	22:10	Earles Sidings – Carlisle London Road	SX	Cement
01:46	7P20,	22;35	Warrington Old Jct – Carlisle Yard	MSX	
03:43	3S24,	23:50	Nottingham – Glasgow Central	MX	Parcels
06:53	8M72,	03:10	Healey Mills – Carlisle Yard	MX	
07:30	6M75,	05:00	Healey Mills – Ribblehead	SX	Ballast (RR)
07:52	7M86,	20:50	St Blazey – Carlisle Yard	MO	
09:14	5S20,	04:17	Derby – Glasgow Works	MO	Dept. ECS
10:30	**1S49,**	**07:15**	**Nottingham – Glasgow Central**		**Passenger**
10:58	7P08,	06:40	Bescot – Carlisle Yard	MO	
11:06	6M81,	22:30	Llandeilo Jct – Carlisle Yard	MSX	ABS
11:31	6M81,	01:05	Severn Tunnel Jct – Carlisle Yard	MO	ABS
11:46	7P08,	05:42	Bescot – Carlisle Yard	MSX	
12:36	8M18,	07:25	Tinsley – Carlisle Yard	SX	(WC)
13:51 (X)	**1S68,**	**10:31**	**Nottingham – Glasgow Central**		**Passenger**
14:04	7M86,	20:50	St Blazey – Carlisle Yard	MSX	
15:02	7M49,	05:50	Severn Tunnel Junction – Carlisle Yard	MO	
17:33	8M64,	12:35	Healey Mills – Carlisle Yard	SX	
19:17	**1S85,**	**16:05**	**Nottingham – Glasgow Central**		**Passenger**
21:48	7M14,	19:00	Healey Mills – Carlisle Yard	SX	
22:22	7P28,	14:15	Bescot – Carlisle Yard	SX	

Notes :
1.	(WC)	Stops at Blea Moor signal box to set down / pick up water cans
2.	(RR)	Loco runs round at Blea Moor
3.	ABS	Air Brake Service
4.	(X)	Former "Thames-Clyde Express"

Anglo - Scottish Expresses

Until 1982, there were three Anglo-Scottish express trains over the 'S & C' each way, running between Glasgow Central and Nottingham. Most of these were hauled by a Class 45/1 or Class 47/4 loco, fitted with ETH (Electric Train heating) equipment.

On 3rd June 1980, the driver of Class 45/1 No.45108 (above) piles on the power as 1M86, the 11:50 Glasgow Central - Nottingham passes through Garsdale; 1M86 being the old 'Thames Clyde Express'.

Meanwhile, three days later, another Toton based loco (allocated from Immingham in May 1980) Class 47/4 No.47552 (below) bursts out of the north portal of Blea Moor tunnel with 1S49, the 07:15 Nottingham - Glasgow Central; the first northbound passenger service of the day.

Note the Banner Signal guarding the entrance to the tunnel, an invention of W R Sykes & Co around 1900. Electronically operated from Blea Moor signal box, the "arm" of the signal rotated on an opaque disc in a glass case, like a semaphore signal. This one has since been replaced by a colour light signal.

Trains In Trouble ....

The signalman at Garsdale looks on, as Class 40 No.40050, piloting an ailing No.40019 (above), finally passes his 'box with a very late running 7M86, St. Blazey - Carlisle on 3rd June 1980.

Having received the fitter's attention at Carlisle, and already taken a freight south, No.40019 (below) is seen again on the 'S & C', this time coming to the rescue of 'Peak' No.45069 which had failed on 8M18, the 07:25 Tinsley - Carlisle Yard. The train is at Ais Gill summit; the roof of the closed signal box can be seen above the 'Peak' loco and the LMS summit board is to the right of No.40019.

Garsdale

Positioned trackside, close to the southern exit of Moorcock Tunnel, a telephoto lens accentuates the curvature of the track as Class 40 No.40170 (above) crosses Dandry Mire viaduct, Garsdale, on 3rd June 1980 with 7P08, the 07:42 Bescot - Carlisle Yard. The trackbed of the Hawes branch is also in view.

The last freight train I photographed on 4th June 1980 rumbles into Garsdale behind Class 40 No.40178 (below), which is probably 8E15, the 14:43 Carlisle Yard - Healey Mills.

Rise Hill
5th June 1980

A new day and a brisk walk of a mile or so from Dent station to reach a new location, Rise Hill Tunnel.

Without knowing which would come first, it's Class 40 No.40162 (right) storming downhill (1 in 264) towards the tunnel with 6M81, the 22:30 MSX) Llandeilo Jct – Carlisle Yard 'Speedlink', formed mostly of vans.

A quick change of orientation and another centre-panel Class 40, this time No.40171 (middle), rumbles out of the black hole, which is Rise Hill Tunnel, with an unidentified 'up' freight.

On the walk back, I positioned myself about mid-way between Dent station and the tunnel for a shot of 7E84, the 07:30 Carlisle Yard - Tinsley, which duly obliged. Class 45/0 No.45011 (below) is at the head of the train, which includes some 'CSV' Presflo cement tanks in the consist.

If you compare this image with the one of No.66522 on Page 49, the result of tree planting is clear for all to see.

Ais Gill

The familiar outline of Wild Boar Fell is unmistakable, as 'split-box' Class 40 No.40144 (above) prepares for the final push up the 1 in 100 climb to Ais Gill summit on 4th June 1980 with 7E84, the 07:30 Carlisle Yard - Tinsley. Note this Class 40 has had the gangway doors removed from the nose.

The severity of the final few yards to the summit is apparent, as Class 40 No.40170 (below) starts to level off with 6M34, the 06:30 Carlisle London Road - Earles Sidings cement empties. This service is coded 'M', even though it serves a Midland destination. This is due to the train venturing onto eastern metals, two miles east of Skipton, before meeting up again with the Midland Region at Totley in the Hope Valley.

Blea Moor

To relieve the stress on Ribblehead Viaduct, single line working was introduced to prevent two trains from crossing simultaneously, along with a 20mph speed restriction. On 6th June 1980, Class 47/0 No.47229 (above) crawls off the viaduct with 8M18, the 07:25 Tinsley - Carlisle Yard, preparing to stop outside Blea Moor signal box to pick up and set down water cans.

The white flask from Sellafield destined for Hinkley Point nuclear power station, identifies this service as 7V00, the 12:20 Carlisle Yard - Severn Tunnel Junction. The train is hauled by Class 40 No.40185 (below) and, today, nuclear flasks are moved to and from Sellafield, via dedicated services operated by DRS.

Garsdale

On 5th June 1980, Class 40 No.40121 (above) rolls into view at Dent with a heavy 8M64, the 12:35 Healey Mills - Carlisle Yard formed mainly of 2-axle mineral wagons loaded with coal.

It's all over - images such as this one are consigned to history - freight disappeared from the Settle & Carlisle in 1983, air-braked wagonload services replaced unfitted freight trains, Dent signal box and its semaphores were demolished in 1984 and the few remaining Class 40s were all to be withdrawn from traffic in 1985 (No.40122 excepted). It was not to be until 1994 that a freight train would once again turn a wheel in anger over 'S & C' metals, despite the line being saved from closure in 1989.

With this in mind, it's time for me to move on and concentrate on rail travel and, in particular, seeking out rides behind Class 40 locos, preferably over the Settle & Carlisle. For example .....

'S & C' Rail Diary

Personal anecdotes of rail travel over the Settle & Carlisle

First Time - 19th April 1981

Between 15th and 21st April, I was enjoying an 'All Line Railrover' travelling around Scotland and on the East Coast Main Line, seeking out travel behind Class 40s and Class 46 locos.

Whilst travelling behind No.40101 on 2L63, the 21:14 Glasgow Queen Street - Dundee, a fellow enthusiast informed me that the evening's Inverness - London Euston sleeper was 'booked' a Class 40 from Carlisle to Preston, diverted via the 'S & C' due to engineering work on the WCML south of Carlisle. Weekend diversions were commonplace during the winter/spring timetable.

This was an opportunity too good to miss; my first Class 40 over the 'Long Drag'. Together with my two travelling companions from Swindon, we detrained at Dunblane (22:06hrs) and had a 55 minute wait to catch 1M16, the 19:30 Inverness - London Euston; Dunblane was the furthest north we could go to make 1M16.

1M16 departed Dunblane at 23:01hrs, hauled by Class 47 No.47524 to Mossend Yard, where electric traction took over for the run over Beattock to Carlisle, in the shape of Class 83 No.83015, which came to a stop at Carlisle, 02:00hrs on Sunday morning.

.... and there it was, No.40052 'whistling' away in the centre road at Carlisle waiting to take over. These locos were nicknamed 'whistlers' due to the sound of their English Electric traction motors.

Ten minutes later, we were off on the 112 mile journey to Preston; the downside being that there were seven or so sleeping cars between the passenger coach in which I was seated and the loco, so the sound of No.40052 at full power on the climb to Ais Gill could not be enjoyed. However, undaunted, this experience merely whetted my appetite for more!

With Regret .... 17th July 1981

This was the penultimate day of another 'All Line Railrover'; a pre-planned daylight run over the 'S & C' on the former 'Thames Clyde Express' (1M86, the 11:50 Glasgow Central - Nottingham), which changed from electric to diesel traction at Carlisle; hoping for a Class 40, but would likely be a Class 45 'Peak' loco.

Arriving at Carlisle from Berwick upon Tweed behind Gateshead depot's Class 46 No.46039 on 1M04, the 07:18 Edinburgh Waverley - Carlisle, I could see Class 45 No.45043 'The King's Own Royal Border Regiment' stabled, waiting to take over 1M86. During the wait for my train, Landore (Swansea) Class 47 No.47082 'Atlas' arrived with a 'local' express from Glasgow Central via Dumfries and the ex-Glasgow & South Western route. I did not pay much attention to this at the time!

1M86 duly arrived, No.45043 relieved the electric loco, and I boarded the train, making a beeline to the first coach behind the loco. I sat myself down in the first compartment by the window so that I could get a good look at the scenery on our journey south. The train consisted of silver & grey Mark 1 open plan seating and compartment stock, built in the 1950s.

The train departed on time and all seemed well, until five miles into the journey, we came to a stop at Howes Sidings - No.45043 had failed due to a lack of coolant - a replacement loco would have to be summoned from Carlisle Kingmoor / New Yard to rescue the train. No.45043 uncoupled and returned light engine to Carlisle. My immediate thoughts were, perhaps, another 'Peak', or even a Class 40, which would be great.

I then remembered the Class 47 I saw arrive earlier at Carlisle Citadel station, surely they wouldn't send No.47082 to take the train forward. Those people who know me, appreciate how I dislike all things Class 47 and whilst this may seem churlish to others, my worst rail nightmare was about to come true - sure enough, 'control' despatched No.47082 to take the train forward.

I can't tell you how I felt, I could have given up my interest in railways there and then, having to endure more than a 100 miles behind the '47 to Leeds. So it was, but that is only half the tale ....

.... as we proceeded south, I struck up a conversation with a driver and secondman from Carlisle who were travelling in the same compartment to Skipton to pick up a northbound 'S & C' freight. I asked if they were going for 8M64, the 12:35 Healey Mills - Carlisle Yard and they said "yes".

Pulling into Skipton, Class 40 No.40002 was waiting in the 'Down' siding at the head of 8M64 for its new crew. Upon arrival at Skipton, the driver asked "are you coming?" - of course I wanted to, but I thought of all the reasons to say 'NO': the freight would not arrive in Carlisle until after eight o'clock in the evening, I had to get home and what if the railway staff stopped me walking down the track to board the freight train.

Reluctantly, I declined the offer and is a decision I bitterly regret. I can only imagine what a wonderful experience it would have been to travel on a heavily laden freight train over the 'Long Drag' and, there's also the small fact, despite riding behind some 150 different Class 40s, No.40002 always eluded me!

In The Cab - 13th May 1984

I am sure that this particular journey would be the envy of many an enthusiast. Not only was this a daylight run over the 'S & C' but I had the privilege of travelling in the front cab of a Class 40.

The occasion was Sunday, 13th May 1984, on the homeward leg of a three day railtour to the Kyle of Lochalsh and Mallaig, which featured a variety of Scottish-based locos: 20s, 26s, 27s and 37s. Leaving Edinburgh Waverley at 03:00hrs that morning, the return "Skirl o' the Pipes 4" charter to Plymouth (1Z39) was headed by two Class 37s (No.37014 + 37188) for a circuitous amble to Glasgow Central, where they handed over to a pair of Class 20s, No.20110 + No.20154, for the run via the ex-Glasgow & South Western route to Carlisle.

At Carlisle, the 20s detached from the train and two Class 40s, in the shape of 'Celebrity' No.40122 + No.40091 coupled up to the stock ready for the off. I walked up to the leading loco (No.40122) and asked the driver, Eric Richardson of Carlisle Kingmoor depot, if it was possible to have a ride over the 'S & C' and, to my great surprise, he said "yes". I shall not forget climbing the step into the cab as, in my eagerness to get onboard, I bumped my forehead on the door frame, resulting in a thumping great headache for the forthcoming run.

Needless to say, the journey was a memorable experience and I can recall every mile. After a 'photostop' at Dent followed by another one after crossing the viaduct at Ribblehead, I decided to leave the cab at the second stop and travel the rest of the journey back in my seat.

There were many special moments, but three stand out. There's the 'thrash' up to Ais Gill, each loco requiring all of its 2,000 horse power to take 16 coaches up and over the summit; the run through Blea Moor Tunnel in complete darkness with the amazing sound of the locos' engines reverberating off the tunnel walls. Finally, the run over Ribblehead Viaduct, which provided a completely different perspective on the surrounding landscape, the train perched high above the ground on this much maligned structure. I looked out of the cab window to see many heads straining out of the carriage windows for a peep of the locos and scenery, plus the people on the ground frantically waving their arms in warm affection to our passing. Just brilliant.

'40s' on timetabled service trains

21st July 1984

I was at Manchester Victoria station early on this Saturday morning, waiting with other Class 40 enthusiasts to learn what locos were out working this day. The upshot, there was not a single Class 40 I needed a ride behind, although No.40168 was allocated to 1E23, the 10:40 Carlisle - Leeds and 1M26, 15:55 Leeds - Carlisle return; the decision was made, a run over the 'S & C' and an opportunity to clock up 1,000 miles behind No.40168.

I left Victoria station at 07:50hrs behind No.47540 on 1S45, Manchester Victoria - Glasgow Central as far as Preston, where electric loco No.87014 'Knight of the Thistle' took over for the run over Shap to Carlisle, after the Liverpool portion had been added to our train.

No.40168 was already waiting at Carlisle for the run to Leeds and I had a splendid journey in full sun all the way there and back, but it was not until on the return journey (1M26) that No.40168 would amass 1,000 miles as it passed Lazonby & Kirkoswald station. Back at Carlisle, a total of 1,014 miles had been clocked up behind No.'168 and this would prove to be my last journey behind this former Edinburgh Haymarket stalwart.

6th - 10th August 1984

During August 1984, the daily loco-hauled service over the 'S & C' from Carlisle to Leeds (1E23) and return (1M26) was allocated a Class 40 loco. I decided to spend a few days in Carlisle and sample this haulage, which turned out to be shared between Nos.40135 (6th & 7th) and No.40099 (8th & 10th).

My father travelled with me for his 'once only' trip over the 'S & C' on the Monday, hauled by No.40135 to Leeds, where he detrained to return home to Swindon. Unfortunately, for the outward journey, the 'S & C' was fog-bound and my father was thwarted from seeing the splendid scenery through the carriage window.

In total, I made four return trips from Carlisle to Leeds, two each way behind each loco, amassing over 900 miles. You are probably asking what happened on Wednesday, 9th August. Well, I turned up at Citadel station that morning, prepared to take 1E23 to Leeds as planned. However, while waiting for my train, the 'Up' "Royal Scot" (1M05, the 07:55 Ayr - London Euston) arrived hauled by Class 87 No.87012 'Coeur de Lion', which just happened to be the last Class 87 electric loco I needed a ride behind.

So, I declined No.40099 on 1E23 and took a ride behind No.87012 over Shap as far as Preston where, luckily, I fell into another Class 40, No.40013, working 1P11, the 11:15 Liverpool Lime Street - Barrow in Furness and 1K32 return to Crewe. There was no alternative, but a return trip to Barrow!

Those few days spent in the north west of England were very enjoyable, made even more enjoyable by travelling first class, courtesy of British Rail as a thank you for my taking part in a staff training video at British Rail headquarters in Marylebone, London.

(Above) : Class 40 No.40099 is stabled in the carriage sidings, beside 'the wall', at Carlisle Citadel on 9th August 1984 ready to take the stock to a platform and form 1E23, the 10:40 departure to Leeds.

Appendix

Viaducts

Viaduct	Arches	Height (In Feet)	Length (Yards)
HELLIFIELD			
Long Preston			
Settle			
Kirkgate	4	32	55
Settle (Church) / Marshfield	6	45	88
Sheriff Brow	3	55	58
Little	3	25	55
Horton-in-Ribblesdale			
Ribblehead			
Ribblehead	24	104	440
Dent Head	10	100	199
Arten Gill	11	117	220
Dent			
Garsdale			
Dandry Mire / Moorcock	12	50	227
Lunds	5	63	103
Ais Gill	4	75	87
Kirkby Stephen			
Smardale	12	131	237
Crosby Garrett	6	55	110
Griseburn	7	74	142
Ormside	10	90	200
APPLEBY			
Long Marton	5	60	180
Crowdundle	4	55	86
Langwathby			
Little Salkeld	7	60	134
Long Meg / Eden Lacy	7	60	137
Lazonby			
Armathwaite	9	80	176
Armathwaite			
Dry Beck	7	80	139
High Stand Gill / Cotehill	4	91	60
CARLISLE			

(Previous Page) :

On a very warm summer morning, it was quite a trek climbing up the bank to get this view of Dent Head on 10th August 2007. The absence of any freight was a big disappointment but compensation came in the shape of Class 158 unit No.158784 heading south over Dent Head Viaduct with the 08:49hrs Carlisle - Leeds. The train is heading for Blea Moor tunnel in the distance, where the front of another unit can be glimpsed, just about to leave the north portal, with a service from Leeds to Carlisle.   **John Longden**

Miles	Milepost Mileage	Location
	231.20	HELLIFIELD
	232.41	Long Preston
00.00	234.42	SETTLE JUNCTION
1.78	236.40	SETTLE
4.12	238.54	Stainforth Tunnel (South Portal)
4.17	238.59	Stainforth Tunnel (South Portal)
8.01	242.43	Horton-in-Ribblesdale
12.51	247.13	Ribblehead (Down Platform)
12.58	247.20	Ribblehead (Up Platform)
14.63	249.25	Blea Moor Tunnel (South Portal)
16.23	250.65	Blea Moor Tunnel (North Portal)
18.70	253.32	Dent
19.49	254.11	Rise Hill Tunnel (South Portal)
20.24	254.66	Rise Hill Tunnel (North Portal)
22.11	256.53	Garsdale
22.77	257.39	Moorcock Tunnel (South Portal)
23.02	257.44	Moorcock Tunnel (North Portal)
23.76	258.38	Shotlock Hill Tunnel (South Portal)
24.01	258.43	Shotlock Hill Tunnel (North Portal)
25.15	259.57	AIS GILL SUMMIT (1,169ft above sea level)
29.61	264.23	Birkett Tunnel (South Portal)
30.00	264.42	Birkett Tunnel (North Portal)
32.05	266.47	Kirkby Stephen
34.38	269.00	Crosby Garrett Tunnel (South Portal)
34.46	269.08	Crosby Garrett Tunnel (North Portal)
38.51	273.13	Helm Tunnel (South Portal)
38.77	273.39	Helm Tunnel (North Portal)
42.60	277.22	APPLEBY
42.65	277.27	Appleby North Junction
47.40	282.02	Kirkby Thore
50.36	284.78	Culgaith Tunnel (South Portal)
50.66	285.28	Culgaith Tunnel (North Tunnel)
51.06	285.48	Waste Bank Tunnel (South Portal)
51.13	285.55	Waste Bank Tunnel (North Tunnel)
53.61	288.23	Langwathby
57.63	292.25	Lazonby Tunnel (South Portal)
57.68	292.30	Lazonby Tunnel (North Portal)
58.08	292.50	Lazonby & Kirkoswald
61.00	295.42	Baron Wood Tunnel No.1 (South Portal)
61.09	295.51	Baron Wood Tunnel No.1 (North Portal)
61.13	295.55	Baron Wood Tunnel No.2 (South Portal)
61.25	295.67	Baron Wood Tunnel No.2 (North Portal)
62.09	296.51	Armathwaite Tunnel (South Portal)
62.24	296.66	Armathwaite Tunnel (North Portal)
63.47	298.09	Armathwaite
64.63	299.25	Low House Crossing
68.35	302.77	Howe & Co's Sidings
72.50	307.12 / 59.26	Petteril Bridge Junction
72.69	59.45	London Road Junction
73.20	59.76	Carlisle South Junction
73.26	60.02 / 69.09	CARLISLE CITADEL

Acknowledgements

Photographers

My sincere thanks go to all the contributors named below who have kindly supplied images for inclusion in this special edition of 'Line By Line'; a website address is also given, should you wish to see more of these photographers' excellent work.

Name	Website (www.)
Richard Armstrong	richard-armstrong.smugmug.com
Ian Ball	northeastheavy60.uk
Steven Brykajlo	steve-b24.smugmug.com
Ross Byers	flickr.com/photos/47222
Neil Harvey	flickr.com/neil_harvey_railway_photos
Martin Loader	hondawanderer.com
John Longden	johnlongdengallery.photium.com
Kenny Marrs	asterias.co.uk
Dave McAlone	davemcalone.zenfolio.com
Keith McGovern	flickr.com/photos/16359167@N07
Michael McNicholas	(see under Neil Harvey)
James Welham	flickr.com/photos/jameswelham

Bibliography

The Friends Of The Settle - Carlisle set out to actively preserve this unique piece of railway heritage and to improve rail services. Their website contains a wealth of information about the Settle & Carlisle and is worth seeking out:

www.foscl.org.uk

Here's another trainload of coal heading for the Settle & Carlisle, destined for an English power station. On 13th October 2011, FHH Class 66/5 No.66520 (above) approaches Carlisle Citadel station from the north with 6Z68, the 07:02 (TO) Killoch - Cottam loaded coal, complete with pigeon, albeit a dead one, hitching a ride.

Kenny Marrs